Religous Reveries
for Retired Residents

Religous Reveries
for Retired Residents

The impact of the Catholic Church
on the nations of the world.

Albert A. Hoffman, Jr.

Copyright © 2008 by Albert A. Hoffman, Jr.

ISBN:		Softcover		978-1-4363-3719-9

All rights reserved. No part of this book may be reproduced or transmitted in any form or by any means, electronic or mechanical, including photocopying, recording, or by any information storage and retrieval system, without permission in writing from the copyright owner.

This book was printed in the United States of America.

To order additional copies of this book, contact:
Xlibris Corporation
1-888-795-4274
www.Xlibris.com
Orders@Xlibris.com
49482

Contents

Foreword 7

January 2007	Poland—A Reverie	11
February 2007	Italy—A Reverie	24
March 2007	Ireland Reverie	33
April 2007	France Reverie	43
May 2007	Mexico—A Reverie	52
June 2007	Greece—A Reverie	61
July 2007	U.S.A—A Reverie	76
August 2007	China—A-Reverie	87
September 2007	Brazil—A Reverie	100
October 2007	Germany—A Reverie	113
November 2007	India—A Reverie	132
December 2007	Nations and The Catholic Church—A Reverie	146

FORWARD

In December of 2006, the Activity Director of Resurrection Retirement Community (RRC), Rita Goodman, announced that RRC will have an International Year in 2007: "Pack your bags and be ready to visit a variety of countries over the next year. We will be touring many countries of the world right from the comfort of your home. Residents are planning trips, programs, and parties to celebrate and educate us on the customs and cultures of each of the countries we will be visiting. Be sure to check your calendars for all these events. The residents and their committees are hard at work planning events for your enjoyment. A big THANK YOU to them for all they are doing for us. I personally appreciate the efforts they are making in bringing us the best programs available from entertainment to cultural events."

This reflection written by resident Dudley Nee best expresses the success of our International Year: "The food, music, dancing and other activities from the eleven cultures we have celebrated has been an enriching experience for our community. Mass being said in various languages was special. We were also honored to have Mass said by a young African Priest from Zambia. As we think back on these events please join me in thanking everyone who contributed in bringing these highlights to us. We all love our own cultures, but the 'Year' taught us how much we have to treasure in the cultures of others. Hopefully, the more we know and appreciate the 'other guys', and combining with our prayers, make a more peaceful world. It is good to remember that each culture is part of God's family and its followers are our brothers and sisters."

I agreed to Rita Goodman's request to write an article each month on the nation for that month. I was happy to do it! I probably learned more about its culture and history than anyone else, for which I am very grateful.

>   Only the humble are grateful,
>   Only the grateful are happy,
>   Therefore only the humble are happy!

I wish to especially thank two persons without whose help I could not have written these articles. One was Rita Goodman who copy-edited each article. The other was Thomas Zbierski, Director of School Relations, Big Shoulders Fund (Chicago) whose exhaustive research via the internet on the subject nations allowed me to write a readable article. I received from him in a few days a complete and thorough answer to any question I asked him. Again, I wish to thank them both as well as all the others, too numerous to name, for their continuous encouragement and help.

We had several travelogues each month for our subject nation. They showed us the natural beauty of its mountains, hills, waterfalls, rivers, lakes, deserts, plaines, ocean beaches, forests and wild life. Scenes like this certainly inspired all of us but who could express it better than the writer of Wisdom in chapter 13:

> "All men were by nature foolish who were in ignorance of God, and who from the good things seen did not succeed in knowing Him who is, and from studying the works did not discern the artisan; but either fire or wind, or the swift aire, or the circuit of the stars, or the mighty water, or the luminaries of heaven, the governors of the world, they considered gods. Now if out of joy in their beauty they thought them gods, let them know how far more excellent is the Lord than these; for the original source of beauty fashioned them. Or if they were struck by their might and energy, let them from these things realize how much more powerful is He who made them. For from the greatness and the beauty of created things their original author, by analogy, is seen. But yet, for these the blame is less; for they indeed have gone astray perhaps, though they seek God and wish to find Him. For they search busily among His works, but are distracted by what they see, because the things seen are fair. But again, not even these are pardonable. For if they so far succeeded in knowledge that they could speculate about the world, how did they not more quickly find its Lord?"

Now, the Wisdom of Solomon was written about a hundred years before the coming of Christ. The unknown author was a member of the Jewish community at Alexandria and at times spoke in the person of Solomon, placing his teachings on the lips of the wise King of Hebrew tradition in order to emphasize their value. Today, however science has taught us much about the formation of the universe, the earth's processes in its evolution, the design and order of the animal kingdom, etc, in short, the laws of nature, the natural law. But in the nations we studied this year, we were also introduced into the history of these nations and we quickly saw their battles between good and evil. Each of us experienced this same battle in his/her individual life, this battle to do good and avoid evil. Then we most likely eventually saw it in our family, then in our neighborhood, then in our city, then in our state, then in our country, then in our continent, and then finally in our world. Yes like the natural law there is also a moral law that only exists in mankind. Every person in the world was created by God, with a body and a soul made in the image and likeness of this God. We have a memory, an intellect and a freewill. We can choose good or we can choose evil. This is the spiritual warfare that we saw in the citizens of the nations that we read about in our International Year. By now, you might be asking yourself what is this guy talking about? Who knows? I have asked myself this same question many times and I am still learning and searching for answers. As you read through this short book maybe we'll both better understand what I am trying to say. Remember this book is a series of reveries and reveries are very personal. But one thing I am certain of and that is the truth of St. Augustine when he said "You have made our hearts for Thee, O God, and they will be restless until they rest in Thee."

Let's briefly look at a nation's culture and a person's culture and make some observations. Up to one year ago I taught that a nation's culture consisted of its history (50%) and its environment (50%) and that a person's culture consisted of his/her heredity (50%) and his/her environment (50%). I still would teach this. However after studying the eleven nations this year I would suggest that the history of these nations are more or less the same, that's right, the history of these nations are the same, just change the names and the times and the locations, and you will see that their histories read the same way! It should be noted that the environment of these nations depends on their locations on the surface of the earth, ie; on the continents they find themselves, for instance; compare the environment of North America, Central America and South America, all on the same continent; but what different environments for their people. However, their heredity tends to be the same with the passing of time due to wars, immigration, famines, plagues etc. But not so for their individual environment, this is one area of most importance, why, because it directly influences the culture of that person. So we must once again return to the moral law that should govern our environment—do we try to do good and try to avoid evil? Again we recognize the spiritual battle between the forces of good and the forces of evil. And this brings us to Chapter 12 of this book which you will soon read. As of now, I think and I hope I have answered the question I just asked. "What am I talking about?" Ah, gentle and patient reader, I invite you to ponder these words and thoughts during your own reveries and see if you also can answer that question for yourself, "What was I talking about?" Your answer could be very different than mine, but so be it. Before wishing you a Bon Voyage as you continue on your pilgrimage through your own life, I want to remind you of St. Lucy (d304, Virgin and Martyr), the patron saint of sight, upon whom our Lord bestowed the light of faith. Let us venerate her and ask her to increase and preserve this same light in our souls, so that we may be able to avoid evil, to do good and to abhor nothing so much as the blindness and the darkness of evil and sin. Give to us and to our great nation perfect vision to our eyes, that they may serve for your greater honor and glory and for the salvation of souls in this world, so that we may come to the enjoyment of the unfailing light of the Lamb of God in paradise. Now I am ready to end this foreword by wishing you a Bon Voyage through this short book and most of all through your own life ending in Paradise!

Albert A. Hoffman, Jr.

POLAND—A REVERIE

Well, gentle reader, let us begin our International Year of 2007 by touring Poland (Polska), officially the Republic of Poland. Culture—O Yes! Here is a little thumbnail outline. Polish culture has a rich thousand year history influenced from both West and East. Today or tomorrow, we can see these influences in Polish architecture, folklore and art. Poland has been under cultural influence from countries such as Italy, Ottoman Empire, France, our country and most certainly from Chicago! Pope John Paul II, Fryderyk Chopin, Mikolaj Copernicus, Lech Walesa, Henryk Sienkiewicz, Jan Matejko, Marie Curie, Roman Polanski, Witold Gombrowicz and many others including many of you who came from Poland, all influenced the culture of the world.

Poland began to form into a recognizable unitary and territorial entity around the middle of the 10th century under the PIAST dynasty. Poland's first historically documented ruler, MIESZKO 1st, was baptized in 966, adopting Catholicism as the nation's new official religion, to which the bulk of the population converted in the course of the next century. In the 12th century Poland fragmented into several smaller states, which were later ravaged by the Mongol armies of the Golden Horde in 1241. In 1320 Wladyslaw 1st became the King of the reunified Poland. His son, Casimir III repaired the Polish economy, constructed new castles, and won the war against the Ruthenian duchy (LVIV (LWOW) became a Polish City). Under the Jagiellon dynasty, Poland forged an alliance with its neighbor Lithuania. A golden age ensued during the 16th century after the Lublin Union, which gave birth to the Polish-Lithuanian Commonwealth. The citizens of Poland took pride in their ancient freedoms and SEJM Parliamentary system, with the Szlachia nobility enjoying most of the benefits. Since that time Poles have regarded freedom as their most important value; Poles often call themselves the Nation of the Free People.

Poland wrote the first modern constitution in Europe, the Constitution of May 3 in 1791; and the second in the world after out Constitution following our revolutionary war. Recall the great contributions that Count Pulaski and Thaddeus Kosciusko made to our country in our Revolutionary war and later both were active in the writing of Poland's constitution. Sadly, Poland was eventually dissolved after Russia (1772),

Prussia (1793) and Austria (1795) partitioned off all the land of Poland. It would not become a nation again until the end of World War I after the surrender of Germany in November 1918. Poland reaffirmed its independence after a series of military conflicts, the most notable being the 1919-1921 Polish Soviet War. Then came World War II—of all the countries involved in that war, Poland lost the highest percentage of its citizens: over 6 million perished, half of them Polish Jews. Poland also made the 4th largest Allied troops contribution, after the Americans, the British and the Soviets, to ultimately defeat Nazi Germany. World War II started on September 11, 1939 when Nazi Germany and the Soviet Union invaded Poland. Warsaw capitulated on September 28, 1939 and Poland was split into two zones, one occupied by Nazi Germany and the other by the Soviet Union as agreed on in the Ribbentrop-Molotov Pact.

The Battle of Vienna (as distinct from the siege of Vienna in 1529) cannot be overlooked. It took place on September 11 and 12th, 1683 after Vienna had been besieged by Turks for two months. It was the first large-scale battle of the Great Turkish War, yet with the most far-reaching consequences, the most important it saved Christianity from being driven out of Western Europe. A Holy League had been formed to stop the advance of the Ottoman Empire. The Holy League members were Habsburgs, Polish-Lithuanian Commonwealth, Saxony, Bavaria and other allies. A history of these other members would be impossible to relate in the space available here. Suffice it to say that only the Polish-Lithuanian Commonwealth volunteered to take over the command; he was King John III Sobieski and he was made commander-in-chief of his own 30,000-man Polish forces and of the 40,000 troops of Habsburg and their allies, led by Charles V, Duke of Lorraine. These 70,000 men were pitted against the Ottoman army of approximately 138,000 men under the command of Grand Vizier Kara Mustafa Pasha.

On 6th September, 1683, the Poles crossed the Danube 30KM northwest of Vienna to unite with the Imperial forces of Austria and additional troops from Saxony, Bavaria, Baden, Franconia and Swabia who had answered the call for a Holy League that was supported by Pope Innocent XI. The relief army had to act quickly to save Vienna from the Turks. Despite the international composition and the short time of only six days, an effective leadership structure was established indisputedly centered on the King of Poland, John III Sobieski and his heavy cavalry. The motivation was high, as this war was not one that was for the interests of kings, but one that was for the entire Christian faith; and unlike the crusades, the battleground was in the heart of Europe! The Holy League forces arrived on the "Kanlen Berg" (bare hill) above Vienna, signaling their arrival with bonfires. In the early morning hours of 12 September, before the battle, a mass was held for King Sobieski. After 12 hours of fighting, Sobieski's Polish force held the high ground. Four cavalry groups, one of them Austrian-German and the other three Polish, totaling 20,000 men, charged down the hills. The attack was led by Sobieski in front of a spearhead of 2,000 heavily armed winged Polish lancer hussars. This charge broke the lines of the Ottomans, turned the tide of battle against them and their defeat. In less than three hours after the cavalry attack, the Christian forces had won the battle and saved Vienna from capture. The Turks lost about 15,000 men in the fighting, compared to approximately 4,000 for the Habsburg-Polish forces. The battle of Vienna is seen by many historians as marking the beginning of the decline of the Ottoman Empire. The battle also marked the historic end of Turkish expansion into southeastern Europe. In honor of Sobieski, the Austrians erected a church atop a hill of Kahlenberg, North of Vienna. The train route from Vienna to Warsaw is also named in Sobieski's honor. The constellation Scutum Sobieskii (Sobieski's shield) was named to memorialize the battle. Because Sobieski had entrusted his kingdom to the protection of the Blessed Virgin (Our Lady of Czestochowa) before the battle, Pope Innocent XI commemorated his victory by extending the feast of the Holy Name of Mary to the Universal Church, which until then had been celebrated solely in Spain and the Kingdom of Naples, to the universal Church; it is celebrated on September 12. Several culinary legends are related to the battle of Vienna:

1. The croissant was invented in Vienna in 1683 to celebrate the defeat of the Turkish siege of the city, as a reference to the crescents on the Turkish flags.
2. The first bagel as being a gift to King John (Jan) Sobieski to commemorate the king's victory over the Turks that year. The baked-good was fashioned in the form of a stirrup, to commemorate the victorious charge of the Polish cavalry.
3. After the battle, the Austrians discovered many bags of coffee in the abandoned Turkish encampment. Using this captured stock, Franciszek Jerzy Kulezycki opened the third coffeehouse in Europe and the first in Vienna, where according to legend, Kulezycki himself or Amarco d'Aviano, the Capuchin Friar and confidant of Leopold I, Holy Roman Emperor, added milk and honey to sweeten the bitter coffee, thereby inventing cappuccino.

4. When the Turks were pushed away from Vienna, the military bands left their instruments on the field of battle and that is how the Holy Roman Empire (and the rest of "Western" countries) acquired cymbals, bass drums and triangles.

As you have read Poland was no more from 1793 until 1918, but the love of freedom still beat in the hearts of the Poles. One such Pole was Bogdan Janski, a layman. He was born March 26, 1807 in Lisowo, Poland and died on July 2, 1840 in Rome, Italy; a professor of economics, a fervent patriot, a voluntary exile, a man of the deep interior change, conversion and spiritual resurrection, a public penitent, a lay apostle of the Polish emigration in France, an educator of priests. He proclaimed loud and clear: "Poland will rise again"; and indeed it did. Bogdan Janski, Peter Semenenko, CR, and Jerome Kajsiewicz founded the Congregation of the Resurrection (A.K.A. Resurrectionists and CR's) and what a gift to the world especially to Chicago they have been.

Recall also that Poland's days of greatness as a nation coincided with the Renaissance in Europe, hence the architecture of the majority of Polish Churches in Chicago are classical Renaissance or Baroque. Incidentally, the Chicago World's Fair of 1893 revived interest in classical forms. The magnificent Basilica of Our Lady of Sorrows showed this classical influence.

The Polish churches built along the Milwaukee Avenue corridor reflected the Renaissance glory of Polish Catholicism. St. Mary of the Angels, (1914-20) with a soaring dome to rival St. Peter's in Rome, is the ultimate example of the Polish Renaissance style. Fr. Francis Gordon, the first pastor of the parish beginning in 1899 and a leading member of the Polish Resurrectionist order, commissioned this building as a Polish Cathedral. This church testifies to the generosity of its parishioners. Sadly, it deteriorated over the years and was closed for a time and threatened with demolition; but heroic fundraising efforts by its past and present parishioners allowed it to reopen in 1992. Resurrection priests and sisters continue to serve the parish and neighborhood. There are at least 20 Polish churches in Chicago and most of them designed in the beautiful Polish Renaissance style.

Archbishop George W. Mundelein in his dedication sermon in 1920 of St. Mary of the Angels compared its construction to the great Cathedrals of Rheims, Amiens and Cologne, noting that "the people in this neighborhood were satisfied to contribute from their slender earnings in order that God's house might rise gigantic, majestic and beautiful, while about it clustered their poorer and unpretentious homes . . ." the Bishop congratulated the parishioners of St. Mary of the Angels as he continued "for among all of the churches of this great city, they have added one of the most beautiful. It will stand here as a monument of the zeal, the deep faith and the generous spirit of self-sacrifice of the children of the Polish race in this city . . ."

But St. Hyacinth Church (1917-21), Polish Renaissance style, seating 2,000, must be highlighted. The three cupolas on it towers which rise high above the Avondale neighborhood are a witness to the faith of the Polish Catholics who built it and St. Hyacinth continues to be a thriving parish today. It was founded by Rev. Vincent Barzynski, C.R. from St. Stanislaus Kostka parish in 1894. The interior of the church is huge, but at the principal masses on Sunday all the seats are occupied, the two balconies are full, there is standing room only in the aisles, and some worshipers must be satisfied to look in through the doors from the sidewalk. Most of these masses are offered in Polish, a few in English. Almost half of the parishioners have come to the United States from Poland. St. Hyacinth parish is under the care of the Resurrection Fathers and the school is operated by the Sisters of the Holy Family of Nazareth.

The second Basilica in Chicago is All Saints Church. Pope John Paul II elevated St. Hyacinth to a Basilica by proclamation in 2003 and celebrated in St. Hyacinth during November, 2003. Chicago's third Basilica! He gave St. Hyacinth this honor due to the magnificent interior beauty and architecture of this church and to the outstanding devotion of its parishioners. A basilica is the Pope's church in perpetuity consequently there are very few in the United States (between 30 and 35). Chicago has three, very few cities in the world can make this claim!

The Resurrectionists in 1890 founded St. Stanislaus Kostka College on Division Street in Chicago but it was mostly a seminary for young Polish men studying for the priesthood. In 1930 the CR's decided to move the seminary to Kentucky. Later that same year the CR's founded Weber High School for boys in the vacated seminary buildings. The school was named in honor of Archbishop Joseph Weber, CR, who greeted and helped Polish immigrants in the early 1900's. Due to declining enrollment, only 150 students in 1998, the CR's closed Weber in June, 1999. The CR's founded their second high school in September, 1952, Gordon Technical High School, as a College Preparatory High School for the education of youth in the art of technology within a Catholic environment. The curriculum was a thorough blend of religious, academic, cultural, technical and social aspects of life, a unique joining of College Prep and Technical education. Gordon Tech was named after the Very Rev. Francis Gordon, CR (1860-1931). He was known for his diligence in working with immigrants, building his parish (St. Mary of the Angels) and encouraging youth. Rev. John Dzielski, CR, was the school's first principal. Over the years, Gordon upgraded its library, added classrooms, won numerous state sports championships, developed the student operated television station—WKGT, hosted President Ronald Reagan, and graduated over 20,000 successful young men. Gordon Tech went co-ed in September, 2002. All throughout the years, Gordon Tech tries to stay grounded in the faith practices that give the members of the Congregation of the Resurrection their life long belief in the risen Lord, the Resurrection of Society. Gordon Tech is still going strong.

Now let's introduce the Sisters of the Resurrection. A widow, Celine Borzecka, and her daughter Hedwig, founded the Sisters of the Resurrection in Rome in 1891.

Central to the mission of the Sisters is the transformation of society with an emphasis on the uplifting of women in that society. The educational ministry of the Sisters in the United States began in 1900 when four sisters came to Chicago and immediately began teaching at St. Mary of the Angels Parish. They soon opened many other schools around Chicago and in other States.

In 1912, Sister Anne Strzelecka purchased over 42 acres of land in northwest Chicago on Old Tanner Road, now Talcott Avenue. A convent and school were built in 1914, and the following year Sr. Anne opened Resurrection Academy, an elementary school and boarding school for girls.

In 1922, Sr. Anne opened the doors to Resurrection High School in what is now the Sisters Provincial home. The first principal was Sr. Antonia Rompkowska, CR (1922-1925), Congregation of the Sisters of the Resurrection. Four years later, the first graduating class consisted of four young women one of whom went on to become a successful attorney, as well as a mother and grandmother of future Resites.

In 1962, Resurrection High School opened its doors at its current location in a new, much larger building. The curriculum program changed and expanded over the following decades to meet the changing needs of young women and to bring it to the strong college preparatory curriculum it provides today.

With its enrollment of approximately 900 young women, receiving many academic awards, many college scholarships, and many sports championships (the Bandits), Resurrection like Gordon tech is also going strong, in fact, very strong!

Our Polish Pope, the great and good John Paul II, Karol Wojtyla, May 18, 1920-April 2, 2005, the vicar of Jesus Christ on earth, was the strongest force in the world for good, forgiveness and peace, both in voice and in action. The world recognized this as attested to by the thousands and thousands who paid their respects and admiration for him at his death, wake and funeral, April 2-10, 2005, regardless of their race, religion, culture, language, or political persuasion. Millions and millions of people around the world could not be there in body but were certainly there in spirit. John Paul II visited Poland many times in his 26 years as Pope (Oct. 16, 1978-April 2, 2005) and communicated with the Polish leaders more times than anyone knows. "The just man appraises the house of the wicked: there is one who brings down the wicked to ruin." John Paul II certainly was the strongest force in bringing down the Soviet Union. He continually encouraged the brave, fearless people of Poland to fight for their freedom, which they did with trust and courage against the communist government in their country. The Soviet Union had instituted a new communist government in Poland, analogous to much of the rest of the Eastern Bloc. Military alignment within the Warsaw Pact throughout the Cold War was also part of this change. In 1948 a turn toward Stalinism brought in the beginning of the next period of totalitarian rule. The People's Republic of Poland was officially proclaimed in 1952. In 1956 the regime became more liberal, freeing many people from prison and expanding some personal freedoms. But persecution of communist opposition figures persisted. Now enter Pope John Paul II in 1978! Labor turmoil in 1980 led to the formation of the independent trade union, "Solidarity" which over time became a political force. It eroded the dominance of the Communist Party; by 1989 it had triumphed in parliamentary elections, and Lech Walesa, a Solidarity candidate eventually won the presidency in 1990. The Solidarity movement greatly contributed to the soon—following collapse of communism all over Eastern Europe. Hoorah for John Paul II! It should be added that the only sculpture of Pope John Paul II in the United States was commissioned by Father Bruno, Pastor of St. Helen (Chicago) in the 1980's, to the number one sculptor in Poland. When it was completed, the sculpture was shipped to St. Helen's and blessed and dedicated by Cardinal George before an overflowing crowd. Incidentally, the construction of St. Helen's began in 1964 at the corner of Augusta and Oakley Boulevards for a contemporary Church in the Polish Parish of St. Helen.

Let us now name and think about some great athletes with Polish roots: Rev. Henry Blaski, CR, Zigmont "Ziggy, DA Mayor," Czarobski, "Bro. Frank" Dusiewicz, CR, Rev. Joe Glab, CR, Rev "Guts" Gutowski, SJ, Stan Hack, Ted Kluzewski, Marie Krajenta, Mike Krzyzewski, Joe Kuzyk, Joe Lesniak, Most Rev. Jerome E. Listecki, Leonard Maryanowski, Stan Mikita, Stan Musial, "Bronco" Nagurski, Ted Perzanowski, Joe Rezotko (minor league baseball hall of fame), Iwona Oleksiar Rog (a member of the Polish National Women's Volleyball team that competed in cities around the world including the U.S.A.), Joe Siwinski, "Moose" Skowron, "Bronco" Telkes, Tom Winiecki, Tony Zale, Tom Zbierski, Rev. Don Zinn, CR.

You can all think of many more you knew about but one thing they all had in common, they were all good Catholics, super athletes, loyal Americans, and all had a special Chicago connection. Pray for all of them were ever they may be.

One of the greatest composers ever was Fryderyk Chopin, (1810-1849), Polish pianist and composer, he had an intense love of freedom. This love shows up in many of his compositions with a strain of sadness and melancholy. No one can ever doubt his love for freedom, especially after listening to his "Revolutionary Etude" and/or his "Polonaise Militaire," both are magnificent and stirring.

But there is another type of music that is equally loved around the world, that being the spirited music of the Polka! How well I remember the days when six of us would jump into my two-tone green Ford and go roaring down the outer drive into lower Wacker Drive and out again roaring to 6300 South Western Avenue, park the car, dash across Western Avenue into Eddie LaRosa's Baby Doll Polka Lounge! What dancing, double-hop Polkas—the best dancers in Chicago. We would dance till closing but the highlight of the evening would always be when Eddie almost extinquished the lights, started his siren screaming through out the room accompanied by his revolving "search" light. You had better be quick and get your drink at the bar because "here comes Eddie" with his squeeze-box dancing up and down the top of the bar! If your drink was there it would end up in your lap. Of course, he was always playing his favorite polka as he went to and fro along the bar—"You are my baby doll" followed by his famous sing-along Polka:

>In Heaven there is no beer
>That's why we drink it here . . .

Boy, what a time we had!! Ah, gentle reader, do I hear your laughter now? So perhaps now is the time to think of all the wedding receptions you attended. They always ended up with the greatest of all polkas—the "Beer Barrel Polka;" Right? Right!!

Let's dance one more polka by remembering the super receptions and banquets we enjoyed at the White Eagle Restaurant and Banquet Hall. What cuisine, what culinary prowess in cooking and baking providing those out-of-this world Polish menus and meals which included Bigos,

Kielbasa, Blintzes, Barszez (Borscht), Czernina (duck blood soup), Schabowy, Kapusta, Pierogi, Paczki, Golabki, various potato dishes and the pastries. Many of the recipes were passed down from generation to generation.

Gadzooks, let's jump into our roadsters now and roar up Milwaukee Avenue to the White Eagle and have a feast to celebrate our first month of our International Year! I'll buy the first "Piwo"!!

Since this is a reverie, let us end this pamphlet with a little more serious tone, that is, with a musing or "getting lost in thought." So, gentle reader, you have heard of many visionaries, mystics, and seers that have appeared in the course of history. Perhaps the best known is the vision that Peter, James and John experienced on Mount Tabor when they saw Jesus transformed before their very eyes into His Divinity talking with Moses and Elijah. Some other visionaries and seers were Teresa of Jesus (1515-1582 Avila), Margaret Mary Alacoque (1674, Paray Le Monial), Bernadette Soubirous (1858, Lourdes) Jacinta and Francisco Marta, Lucia dos Santos (1917, Fatima), Sr. Agnes Sasagawa (c1930. Akita-near Nagasaki). They all experienced a unique vision and message; but all the messages included a request for prayers and penance. Do you remember how in grammar school all our masses ended with the congregation saying special prayers for the conversion of Russia? I wonder why we stopped this and who stopped it? Russia still has not been converted to Christianity.

Do you ever wonder why the Lord selected the Polish nation to be the staunchest defender of Christianity? Since the 15th century Poland has been the most loyal and continuous defender of Christianity. Why do you think the other Christian nations deserted their Christian roots? The Lord selected John Paul II to continue to be the champion of freedom and Christianity as his life most clearly shows. And why did the Lord choose Saint Maria Faustina Kowalska to continue the devotion to His Sacred Heart began by St. Margaret Mary Alacoque by His appearances to her requesting that she introduce His image with two rays emanating from His Heart, one ray red the other blue, with the words "Jesus I trust in You" at the bottom of His image. She was also asked to introduce the Chaplet of the Divine Mercy using the beads of the Rosary and using the words "For the sake of His sorrowful passion, have mercy on us and on the whole world."

Both John Paul II and Benedict XVI have hinted in their encyclical letters that the world could be at the beginning of the last confrontation between good and evil; only time will tell! Back now to Margaret Mary Alacoque. She was chosen by Christ to arouse the church to the realization of the love of God symbolized by the Heart of Jesus. His human heart was to be the symbol of his divine-human heart. By her own love she was to make up for the coldness and ingratitude of the world—by frequent and loving Holy Communion, especially on the First Friday of each month, and by an hour's vigil of prayer every Thursday night in memory of His agony and isolation in Gethsemani. In various appearances to her Jesus manifested His great love for human beings and made 12 promises to those who give particular honor to his Sacred Heart. His 12th promise was "that in the excessive mercy of my heart that my all-powerful love will grant to all those who communicate on the First Friday in nine consecutive months the grace of final repentance; My Divine Heart shall be their safe refuge in this last moment." Why not believe Him? Why don't we continue this reverie by thanking the Lord for all He has given us, especially the Polish Nation and its loyalty to the Church, as part of our Holy Hour every Thursday evening; why don't you, why don't I, why don't we?

Bert Hoffman

ADDENDUM ONE TO POLAND—A REVERIE, January, 2007

This article was entitled POLAND, written by Jadwiga Antonczyk, a resident at RRC. It was published in our monthly publication, 'Phoenix', issued in January, 2007.

Albert A. Hoffman, Jr.

POLAND
By: Jadwiga Antonczyk

International year, 2007, this year at RRC some of our residents of foreign decent, now American citizens will talk about the countries they and their ancestors came from. The biggest group of Polish-American residents is privileged to be the first to talk and share our history.

Poland existed since 960. The first Polish King, Mieszko 1st, united the tribes of pagans in one unit in the western part of Poland. He was baptized in 966, and the country accepted the Christian faith.

From the year 960 until 1795, Poland was ruled by 49 Kings. During this time they were fighting for different reasons against Germans, Russia, Sweden, and Turkey, sometimes losing and sometimes winning. The best and riches times were during the 15th and 16th century. The last King, Stanislaw August Poniatowski signed our first Constitution in 1791, which was also the first constitution in Europe. Russia did not approve of it and demanded elimination of it. One year later in 1792, part of Poland was divided by: Germany, Russia, and Austria. In 1793 and 1795, they took over the rest of Poland. For 123 years our country did not exist.

Both occupants murdered us, filled the prisons with us, tortured us, but we did not give up.

During this time Joseph Pilsudski was a political prisoner in German camps. He was a great patriot and organizer and when he became free he called volunteers to join the army which was named "Legiony". With the army he entered the center of Poland, fought and won our freedom and country. We were free from 1918 until 1939. In those 20 years we tried to rebuild our life. After that time the German army crossed our border on the west, two weeks later Russia did the same in the east. It was September 1st, 1939 when they divided Poland among themselves. In the beginning, we were disoriented—not knowing what to do, but we never gave up—not our freedom—not our beloved Poland. We went underground and the youngest and the oldest joined us—It became the game of "cats and mice."

Both occupants treated us as a piece of dirt, not human beings—everybody heard of the gas chambers in Germany and in occupied Poland where millions died after being tortured and beaten. It happened to small children and very old people—no mercy.

From the eastern art of Poland, occupied by Russia, we were deported to Siberia and the furthest north land, from where there is no return. We all suffered terribly; mostly by the cold temperature which was below 50 degrees, no food, no clothing, and hard work over taxed us. In prison we were tortured, beaten, in the most cruel way, until we bled. When England, USA and the Polish government in exile in London got the news of this they demanded Stalin to meet with them for a discussion.

The document was signed by both sides in 1941, and by this all Polish people who find themselves in Russia for the different reasons, since 1939 must be set free and also that we could have permission to organize a Polish army on their territory and can return to Poland. In 1941, the 2nd Polish corps was organized from the prisoners in Russia. Economy there for years made it hard to stay alive, and impossible to support an army. Again, Stalin was called to another meeting with England, USA and Poland to discuss the Polish army situation. Another piece of paper was singed by them and we had to leave Russia for Iran to watch their oil fields. But before we left the terrible news reached us "Murder in the 'Katyn Forest,' 15,000 Polish soldiers from the P.O.W. camps, professors, doctors, all the best people were shot and than half alive pushed to one big grave with no names and no prayers.

Finally, in April and September 1942 the army and their families left Russia, and through the Middle East finally landed in Italy at the end of 1943. Beginning in 1944 our "2 Polish Corps" became part of the Allied Army.

After landing in Italy we joined the others and moved farther north fighting against Germans. Our field commander General Anders, got the order to conquer Monte Cassino mountain which would open the road to Rome, forcing Germany to run away. The battle began May 11, 1944, and ended in our victory on May 18. This battle is one of the biggest during 2nd World War. This success is noted in history of this war with 2 special chapters of the Polish victory. We were one of the best units among Allied forces. On September 1st 1944, 250,000 soldiers of underground armies were dying during the 68 days of fighting in Warsaw. It was done by children, young and old, men and women, but we lost and were taken to the concentration camps in Germany. A year earlier, our "Air Force Corps" from France, where they were since the beginning of the war together with the British Air Force won the "Battle of England" bringing more honor to our history.

The war in Europe ended May 9, 1945—Hitler lost. Polish armies went to England and from there we could return to Communistic Poland, stay in England, or emigrate to the countries of our choice. Very few ex-soldiers returned home. Some stayed in England and the rest emigrated mostly to the U.S.A., Argentina, and Canada, where we started a new chapter of our life. In U.S.A. we came to Chicago and joined different veteran and fraternal organizations and worked hard. We teach our new generation how to become good American citizens, but always remember Poland and the words on our flag:

"God, Honor and Country"

ADDENDUM TWO TO POLAND—A REVERIE, January 2007

This article entitled "Polish Church Has Chance for Reconciliation" was written by George Weigel in the February 2, 2007 issue of the Catholic New World (Chicago Archdiocese). George Weigel is a senior fellow of the Ethics and Public Policy Center in Washington, D.C.

It's been a tough month for Polish Catholicism. Yet, even in the wake of the resignation of Warsaw's new archbishop and the revelations of clerical cooperation with the communist secret police, the Catholic Church in Poland can reconfirm its traditional roles as the guardian of Poland's noblest instincts and the nation's tutor in moral truth—if it remembers something Pope John Paul II said to a French journalist, Andre Frossard.

Frossard asked, "What is the most important word in the New Testament?" John Paul immediately replied, "Truth." Why? Because the truth sets us free in the deepest meaning of human liberation. And from that spiritual liberation, much good can come. Poland lived that fact of moral and public life in the 1980s, when a revolution of conscience, ignited by John Paul II and supported by the Polish Church, led to the nonviolent Revolution of 1989 and the restoration of Poland's liberties.

Amidst the drama and controversy of the past several weeks, that great truth—"No Church, No Solidarity, No Revolution of 1989"—remains intact. Now, however, the world knows something every Pole, and every serious student of modern Polish history, already knew: not everyone was an anti-communist resistance hero. That fact should not obscure two others, however. First, there were far, far more heroes than scoundrels in polish Catholicism under communism; perhaps 10% of the Polish clergy were involved with the SB, the secret police. Second, the people who produced the SB files now being scrutinized are moral villains, too—as much as, or even more than, those who collaborated, in different ways and with different degrees of culpability.

The Polish Church can regain control of its own story if it provides a comprehensive account of its stewardship during the communist period, using the archive of SB files kept in Poland's Institute of National Memory (IPN). Those materials are "raw files," and some reflect the ambitions of unscrupulous police ferrets more than the truth of particular situations. Yet the IPN archives do contain truths that should be brought to light, both to liberate the Church from burdensome aspects of its past and to confirm the larger truth of the nobility of the Catholic struggle, under extraordinarily difficult circumstances, for the Church's freedom and Poland's. If, in the process, Poles are reminded that moral clarity sometimes lies on the far side of moral complexity, that is no bad thing; it is, in fact, an essential understanding in a democracy. In rendering an account of its stewardship, the Church would also perform a public service. The media is rarely an instrument of precise moral analysis. The Church can help Poles understand that there were different forms of interaction with the SB, and that some activities were far worse than others.

Casual interaction with the ferrets by people seeking passports to study or do research abroad is one thing; others refused even that minimum of cooperation, and their steadfastness should be honored. Still, we have to ask whether someone's interactions with the SB led, with that person's knowledge and will, to material or moral harm to others. Some churchmen—who imagined themselves more clever than the police and accepted advantages in return for clerical gossip—cooperated because of their egos; they strike me more as fools than villains, although their foolishness was not morally neutral. Venality was the sin of others, and a more serious moral failure, too. Those who imagined that they could "use" their secret police contacts to build a more open Polish Church, and ended up doing the communists' political bidding, bear a particularly heavy burden; they betrayed both Church and society.

The kind of comprehensive, carefully calibrated moral reckoning needed here can only be provided by the polish Church itself, in cooperation with reputable scholars. During the years I've been aware of the IPN archives, I've been waiting for the Polish Church to seize what struck me as a great opportunity. It didn't; the result is the drama and damage of the past month. Yet the opportunity remains. In the spirit of John Paul II who taught the liberating power of truth, it should be seized—quickly.

February 3, 2007

ITALY—A REVERIE

Ciao! The history of Italy and its people starts some 200,000 years ago, yes, that's right, the "Old Stone Age." So that's all that will be said on Italy's history save for a few facts that Italy has influenced the cultural and social development of the whole Mediterranean area, deeply influencing European culture as well. As a result, it has also influenced other important cultures. The unification of Italy was finally obtained on March 17, 1861 under their leader Giuseppe Garibaldi. Vittorio Emanuele II became the first King of the United Italy. The Fascist dictatorship of Benito Mussolini lasted from 1922 to 1943. In 1929 Mussolini lasted from 1922 to 1943. In 1929 Mussolini realized a Pact with the Holy See, resulting in the rebirth of an independent state of the Vatican for the Catholic Church in the heart of Rome as it still is today. Italy was invaded by the Allied Forces in 1943 and in September 1943 Italy surrendered. It was immediately invaded and occupied by military forces and became the theatre of a savage civil war between freedom fighters and Nazi and Fascist troops. The country was finally liberated by a national uprising on 25 April 1945 (The "Liberazione"). Italy is a founding member of the European community, European Union and NATO.

Italy has been a seminal place for many important artistic and intellectual movements that spread through out Europe and beyond, including the Renaissance and Baroque. Its long artistic heritage is validated through the names of Michelangelo, Leonardo DaVinci, Donatello, Botticelli, Fra Angelico, Tintoretto, Caravaggio, Bernini, Titian and Raphael, among many others. There is no shortage of its literary figures: Dante Alighieri, Boccacio, Giacomo Leopardi, Alessandro Manzoni, Tasso, Ludovici Ariosto, and Petrarca, whose best known vehicle of expression, the Sonnet, was invented in Italy. Prominent philosophers include Bruno, Ficino, Machiavelli, Vico, and in science, Galileo Galilei who made considerable advancements toward the scientific revolution, and Leonardo da Vinci was the Quintessential Renaissance man. Other notable Italian scientists and inventors include Fermi, Cassini, Volta, LaGrange, Fibonacci, Marconi, and Meucci. From folk music to classical, music has always played an important role in Italian culture. The piano and violin were invented in Italy. Some of Italy's most famous composers include Palestrina and Monteverdi (Renaissance), Corelli and Vivaldi (Baroque), Paganini and Rossini, (classical), Verdi and Puccini (Romantic), Berio and Nono (experimental). Space will not allow more than brief sketches of four outstanding Italians, although there are many more that impacted the world including the United States.

(1.) Christopher Columbus (1451-1506) insisted on bringing Franciscan and Dominican missionaries with him in 1492 to the New World. This was pivotal to the spread of Catholicism among the natives in North, Central and South America. He knew the world was not flat and since Marco Polo's land route to China was becoming more and more dangerous and expensive, he convinced King Ferdinand and Queen Isabella of Spain to fund the expedition to secure Spain's wealth (Ferdinand's goal) and to evangelize and spread the Catholic faith (Isabella's dream). Before setting sail on the Nina, Pinta, and Santa Maria, Columbus went to confession and mass, and he received Holy Communion. His flagship had a chapel where mass was offered daily. Today, the Chapel's altar is in Boalsburg, Pennsylvania, at the Christopher Columbus Museum. Keep in mind that 1492 was still the middle ages. The reformation wouldn't occur for another 15 years. Unlike Cortez, Columbus didn't see native Americans as slaves or enemies but as potential converts to and allies of Catholic Spain.

(2.) On the morning of February 20, 1878, the papal conclave elected Joachim Pecci as the new pope who took the name Leo XIII (1878-1903). Without a doubt, Leo's most significant contribution was in his pronouncements in the social realm. At this time the Industrial Revolution was in full swing in England, Germany, and our country. The common rights of workers were threatened and denied. As a result, Pope Leo wrote the magnificent papal encyclical RERUM NOVARUM (1891) on the sanctity of human work, dignity of workers, and the justice that's owed to them. He condemned all sorts of radical stances, such as extreme capitalism and atheistic communism, while defending the rights of private property and the right to form guilds or trade unions. This social encyclical gave the impetus for Catholic unions in our country. Leo died on July 20, 1903, at the age of 93, the first pope whose passing was mourned not only in churches and convents but in factories and union halls. Even today, any lawyer who is involved in labor/management disputes starts his study with the reading of RERUM NOVARUM. In 1889 Pope Leo XIII sent Sister Maria Francesca Cabrini (1850-1917), founder of the Missionary Sisters of the Sacred Heart (1877 in Italy) to our country to work with Italian immigrants. In 1946 she became the first American citizen to be canonized. Her congregation has spread throughout the U.S., Italy, South and Central America and England. Here is a quote of St. Frances Cabrini: "We must pray without tiring, for the salvation of mankind does not depend on material success; nor on sciences or arms and human industries, but on Jesus alone."

(3.) Pope St. Pius X, 1903-1914 (Giuseppi Sarto) followed the reign of Leo XIII. He was known as the Pope of the children. He extended the right to receive Holy Communion to all Catholic children who had reached the age of reason—7 years old. Also, he composed a syllabus of errors. In it he condemned certain tenets of "Modernism," a heresy that denied aspects of the faith and accepted all sorts of progressivism to the point that damaged the integrity of the faith. This implied that you were a modern thinker and able to communicate this to your contemporaries. Rather, to get its message across, modernism used falsehoods to prove its point. If anything, modernism was nothing more than elaborate academic skepticism run rampant.

(4.) The church was unanimously against the evils of communism on the one hand and fascism on the other. With the onslaught of World War II, Pope Pius XII, 1939-1958 (Eugenio Pacelli) diplomatically tried to help those affected by the diabolical evil of Adolph Hitler. Though maligned by some in the secular press today, Pius XII actively worked for the safety of the Jewish people. Shortly after his election as Pope (March 2, 1939), the Nazi newspaper, "Berliner Morgan Post" blasted: "The election of Cardinal Pacelli (as Pius XII) is not accepted with favor in Germany, because he was always opposed to Nazism." At one point during the war, the Vatican, considered neutral territory by the Geneva Conference, hid and cared for 3,500 Jews. Through its Nuncios (ambassadors), the Chruch 3 falsified documents to aid Jews by providing fictitious baptismal certificates to appear as Catholic Christians. As a result, many priests, nuns, Catholic laymen lost their lives rescuing and sheltering their brother and sister Jews. Recently released Vatican records indicate that the Catholic Church operated an underground railroad that rescued 800,000 Euopean Jews from the holocaust. In 1942, The New York Times editorial (December 25) read:

> The voice of Pius XII is a lonely
> voice in the silence and darkness
> enveloping Europe this Christmas . . .
> he is about the only ruler left on the
> Continent of Europe who dares to
> raise his voice at all.

Finally, in 1958, Prime Minister Golda Meir sent a moving eulogy at the death of Pope Pius XII:

> We share in the grief of humanity . . .
> when fearful martyrdom
> came to our people, the voice of
> the pope was raised for its victims.
> The life of our times was enriched
> by a voice speaking out about
> great moral truths above the
> tumult of daily conflict. We mourn
> a great servant of peace.

The most eloquent testimony to the real Pius XII who did all he could to help save Jews during World War II is the conversion of the Chief Rabbi of Rome, Israele Anton Zolli, to Roman Catholicism in 1945 in appreciation. He even took the baptismal name Eugenio, because it was Pius XII's baptismal name.

Right now I wish to thank and acknowledge the help I received from my friend Reverend John Trigilio, Jr. co-author of "Catholicism for Dummies." Father Trigilio is a co-host of two weekly TV series on the Eternal Word television network (EWTN): 'Web of Faith' and 'Council of Faith'.

ADDENDUM ONE: Church growth in a crumbling empire (400-700). This history obviously greatly exceeds the scope of this reverie but fortunately there are many books available on this subject. Also, to better understand the following paragraphs obtained from "The Catholic Church: Our Mission in History" (pages 128-131) by Pluth and Koch, it might be helpful for you to read these brief comments on names mentioned in these paragraphs.

(1.) Clovis (466-511) Frankish King (481-511, Merovingian Dynasty). A pagan tribe, the Franks lived north of the Rhine River in an area that would now include parts of Germany, Holland, Belgium, and France. In 496, Clovis was baptized by Bishop Remy at Rheims. Three years earlier Clovis had married a Christian princess who taught him much of the faith. Following the customs of the times, about three thousand of his soldiers received baptism with him. Among all the nomadic tribe along the Rhine, the Franks were the only ones Catholic, the rest were still Arians. Soon, Arianism began to die out in the western part of the empire.

(2.) Theodoric the Great (454-526) King of the Ostrogoths (474-526). In 493, Theodoric began his thirty-six year rule of Italy. He gave his retiring soldiers land in Italy, and so they settled alongside the Romans. He granted religious freedom to all. He realized that in Italy the Church alone had the organization needed to keep a large body of people peaceful. Even as an Arian, he did not hesitate to ask Catholic Bishops to help him solve the empire's problem. During his long reign Theodoric ruled justly. Thus Italy and the Church experienced some years of relative peace.

(3.) Conditions improved under Clovis in Gaul and under Theodoric in Italy, but no one knew when danger would again rise. The Church had problems too. Disagreements arose between the Bishop of Rome and the Patriarch of Constantinople, who was allied to the Eastern emperor. Pope Gelasius (492-496) assigned a number of theological questions and matters of liturgical practice to a very capable monk named Denis the Short, one of the few scholars who knew both Latin and Greek. His decisions were the beginnings of Canon Law or Church Law. He started a new calendar to replace the one that had been used in the Roman Empire for more than a thousand years. Instead of counting the years from the founding of Rome, Denis began the dating from the year of Christ's birth, the system we use today. Christians accepted this new calendar as a daily reminder that Jesus Christ is the center of all time.

(4.) Benedict (480-543). It is unfortunate that no cotemporary biography was written of a man who has exercised measureless influence on monasticism in the West. Benedict was born of a distinguished family in central Italy, studied at Rome and early in life was drawn to the monastic life. At first he became a hermit, leaving a depressing world: Pagan armies on the march, the Church torn by schism, people suffering from war, morality at a low ebb. He soon realized that he could not live a hidden life in a small town any better than in a large city, so he withdrew to a cave high in the mountains for three years. Some monks joined him and the shift from hermit to community life had begun for him. He had an idea of gathering various families of monks into one "Grand Monastery" to give them the benefit of unity, fraternity, permanent worship in one house. Finally he began to build what was to become one of the most famous monasteries in the world, Monte Cassino, commanding three narrow valleys running toward the mountain. Now to Pluth and Koch!

Benedict

While Clovis was building the kingdom of the Franks in Gaul and while Theodoric the Goth was ruling Italy, a young man named Benedict was studying law in Rome. Before he finished his studies, at about age twenty, Benedict became disgusted with the sin, crime, and confusion that seemed to exist everywhere.

Like Antony and the monks before him, Benedict became disgusted with the sin, crime, and confusion that seemed to exist everywhere. Like Antony and the monks before him, Benedict wanted to seek God in the silence of the countryside. So he left Rome and joined a religious group living about thirty miles from the city. A short time later, he took another step and became a hermit—living alone in a mountain cave. At last, he had the solitude he desired.

His lone existence did not last long. People began to come to Benedict seeking his advice and prayers. Eventually a group of monks came to ask him to be their superior. They wanted to be good monks but found it hard to order their lives in such a way that they could balance prayer, meditation, work, and service. Unfortunately this first group was insincere, and within a short time resented Benedict's attempts to give them direction. Soon he was back in his cave alone with God. Before long, another group came to seek his guidance. This group followed Benedict's advice and became the nucleus of his first monastery.

In the year 530 on top of Monte Cassino—about halfway between Rome and Naples—Benedict and his monks built the center of Western monasticism. The community was composed of ordinary people, converted Goths and Romans. Bendict taught them how to read so that they could understand the Scriptures and the prayers said each day. Their lives were simple and well ordered, balanced between "prayer and work"—in Latin, ora et labora. The community within the monastery at Monte Cassino was nearly a complete economic unit, supplying itself with food, clothing, and shelter. In its quiet scriptorium, monks copied sacred books and preserved secular books containing the writings of famous authors. At Monte Cassino, Benedict wrote what came to be called the Benedictine Rule—which eventually became the basic guide for religious life and discipline in communities throughout the Western world.

Though the points of the Rule came from his own experience and immense common sense, Benedict realized that he was building on a tradition that was centuries old—a tradition begun by Antony, the hermit living in the deserts of Egypt. He may also have contemplated the sample rule written by Basil for the monks in Asia Minor. Jerome had lived as a monk in Bethlehem and had organized several monasteries. Even Augustine had written a short set of guidelines for the religious community that he began in his North African hometown. Patrick too had established monasteries in Ireland. Nonetheless, Benedict's Rule became recognized as the most inspired description of monastic life.

Selections from Saint Benedict's Rule

* A monastery ought, if possible, to be so constructed as to contain within it all necessaries—that is, water, mill, garden, and places for the various crafts . . . so that there will be no occasion for monks to wander abroad.

* A mattress, a coverlet, a pillow are to suffice for bedding.
* There (should) be at all seasons of the year (two) cooked dishes, so that he who happens not to be able to eat of the one may make his meal of the other. . . . "Take heed to yourselves lest perhaps your hearts be overcharged with (indulgence)."
* Although we read that "wine is not the drink of monks at all," yet, since in our day they cannot be persuaded of this, let us at least agree not to drink to excess but sparingly. A pint of wine a day is sufficient for anyone.
* When the brothers rise for the Divine Office, let them gently encourage one another, because of the excuses made by those who are drowsy.
* Let all guests who come be received as Christ would be . . . . As soon, therefore, as a guest is announced let him be met by the prior or the brethren, with all marks of charity . . . . Let special care be taken of the poor and pilgrims, because in them Christ is more truly received . . .
* Let there be stationed at the gate of the monastery some wise old man who knows how to give and receive an answer, and whose age will not allow him to wander from his post . . . . As soon as any one shall knock, or some poor man shall call for help, let him reply, "Thanks be to God," or invoke a blessing.

The Monk's Day at Monte Cassino—Prayer and Work

Quietly a robed figure moves about a chilly dormitory filled with sleeping men; the sound of a bell is heard as this monk summons his brothers to Nocturns—the first of seven periods of prayer each day. It is 2:00 a.m. The monks rub the sleep from their eyes, silently gather themselves together and file into the chapel. The monks meditate while waiting for the leader to intone the start of Nocturns. The simple melodies of the chant flow through the stone church. When Nocturns is completed, the monks make their way back to their wooden cots for another hour or so of sleep. Before six, with the sun, they are back in chapel for Lauds. Leaving chapel, they spend some time in private reading and meditation before meeting back in chapel for Prime. A simple breakfast is eaten just before a period of morning work. Each brother has jobs to do according to his ability and the needs of the monastery. These men do not mind; most of them are simple men from the countryside—if they were laymen, most would be farmers or do some other kind of hard labor. Besides, to them prayer and work are one. At 9:00 a.m. Terce is sung, and the monks celebrate the Eucharist. All join in the singing because "he who sings prays twice."

Mass done, another period of manual labor follows. Right before noon, Sext is chanted, and lunch is eaten. It is a plain meal of vegetables and bread, accompanied by a little ordinary wine. By this time the monks are ready for a brief siesta or nap. At 3:00 p.m. they are gathered in chapel for None. After this they head for the fields to tend the crops, for the tailor shop to sew new robes, for the scriptorium to copy books, or for the bakery to prepare the sturdy bread for the monks and the frequent beggars and pilgrims who appear at their gate; there are numerous jobs to be done if the monastery is to sustain itself. At 6:00 p.m. they are once more chanting the Psalms and listening to the Word of God during Vespers; the light meal they have just had has a chance to digest. They are content in this period before the close of their day. Like most of their lives, the short time for private reading and meditation is spent silently in the presence of God. Compline is sung right before they head to the dormitory and their much-deserved rest.

The followers of Saint Benedict have worked about six hours, slept about eight hours and prayed together about three hours. The rest of the day is spent in spiritual reading and meditation; even meals are eaten silently while inspirational texts are read by a brother monk. They have praised God with their heads, hearts, and hands. Some might call it a hard life, but not these men. The only hard life for them would be life away from the presence of God so apparent in Monte Cassino.

Monte Cassino was the scene of a vicious battle in World War II. In October, 1942, a British army under General Bernard Montgomery defeated the Germans and Italians at EL ALAMEIN, Egypt, and began puruing them westward. In November, 1942, an Anglo-Canadian-American army under General Dwight D. Eisenhower invaded French North Africa and moved eatward. By thus placing the enemy in a vise, the Allies destroyed the Axis African armies. In 1943 the Allies crossed the Mediterranean and invaded Sicily and southern Italy. Mussolini's Fascist government collapsed, and Italy surrendered unconditionally. To resist the Allied advance northward, Germany rushed troops into Italy. The Germans selected the monastery at Monte Cassino to be their strongest military resistance. Fortunately the monks had several days to bury or relocate their most ancient and precious artifacts before the Allied air attacks began. After a few days of continuous bombings the monastery was completely destroyed, the Allied ground forces then moved up the mountain into the heavy gunnery of the Germans dug in bunkers along the mountain top. The death toll was awful on both sides. Monte Cassino finally fell. Stiff German resistance held the Allies back many months in Italy, but at length, on June 4, 1944, Rome was taken. Today the monastery is once again very active and has been completely restored to its former grandeur including all its ancient and precious artifacts!

ADDENDUM TWO TO ITALY—A REVERIE

Let's end this reverie with a few words about the most famous Basilica in Rome. November 9TH celebrates the dedication of the cathedral church of Rome (the Pope's local parish as Bishop of Rome) by Pope Sylvester I in 324.

Originally called the Most Holy Savior, it is called St. John Lateran because it was built on property donated by the Laterani family and for its baptistry named after St. John. It has withstood barbarian attacks, earthquakes and fire to provide a residence for popes through the centuries. In the late 1500s Pope Clement VIII commissioned a baroque renovation. The present façade was completed in 1735. May we celebrate our unity today with this church that is "the mother and head of all churches of the city and of the world" (omnium ecclesiarum Urbis et Orbis mater et caput).

Also at this time lived St. Ambrose (339-397) who as a Roman governor mediated a disputed Episcopal election in Milan (370) and was acclaimed bishop by the people although he was not yet baptized. He excelled as preacher, teacher, and pastor. He influenced the conversion of St. Augustine, whom he baptized (386). He was named one of the four great doctors of the Latin church (1298). May we say with him, "thanks be to the Gospel, by means of which, we also who did not see Christ when He came into this world seem to be with Him when we read His deeds. Prayer is the wing by which the soul flies to heaven, and meditation the eye by which we see God."

IRELAND—A REVERIE

Ireland was mostly ice-covered and joined by land to Britain and continental Europe during the last ice age. It has been inhabited for about 9000 years. Stone age inhabitants arrived sometime after 8000 BC. The Bronze Age, which began around 2500 BC saw the production of elaborate gold and bronze ornaments and weapons. The Iron Age in Ireland is associated with people now known as CELTS. The Romans referred to Ireland as Hibernia. Ptolemy in AD 100 records Ireland's geography and tribes. Native accounts are confined to Irish poetry, myth, and archaeology. Those who would like more on Ireland's history should visit the many Chicago museums that include much on this history. But it must be mentioned that history maintains that in AD 432, St. Patrick arrived on the island and in the years that followed worked to convert the Irish to Christianity. The Druid tradition collapsed in the face of the spread of the new faith. Monasteries flourished especially in the arts of manuscript illumination, metalworking and sculpture producing such treasures as the Book of Kells, ornate jewelry, and the many carved stone crosses that dot the island. This era was interrupted in the 9th century by 200 years of intermittent warfare with waves of Viking raiders who plundered monasteries and towns. Eventually they settled in Ireland and established many towns, including the modern cities of Dublin, Cork, Limerick and Waterford. Again, visit a museum or a library to read about the English taking control of the whole Island. After the Irish Rebellion of 1641, Irish Catholics were barred from voting or attending the Irish Parliament. The new English Protestant ruling class was known as the PROTESTANT ASCENDANCY. The history of the bitter wars between Ireland and Northern Ireland is readily accessible.

In more recent times, Ireland has produced four winners of the Nobel Prize for Literature: George Bernard Shaw, William Butler Yeats, Samuel Beckett and Seamus Heaney. Although not a Nobel Prize winner, James Joyce is widely considered one of the most significant writers of the 20th century. His 1922 Ulysses is sometimes cited as the greatest English-language novel of the 20th century and his life is celebrated on June 16th in Dublin as the Bloomsday celebration.

A ring of coastal mountains surrounds low central plains. The island is bisected by the River Shannon. The island's lush vegetation, a product of its mild climate and frequent but soft rainfall, earns it the sobriquet "Emerald Isle." The island's area is 32,591 square miles.

Ireland's largest religious group is the Catholic Church (about 70% for the entire island). The largest Protestant denomination is the Anglican Church of Ireland. The Irish Muslim community is growing, mostly through increased immigration. The island has a small Jewish community, although this has declined somewhat in recent years. Since joining the European Union in 2004, Polish people have been the largest source of immigrants (over 120,000) from central Europe, followed by other migrants from Lithuania, Czech Republic and Latvia.

It is Ireland's high standard of living, high wage economy and EU membership that attract many migrants from the newest of the European Union countries: Ireland has had a significant number of Romanian immigrants since the 1990's. In recent years mainland Chinese have been migrating to Ireland in significant numbers. Nigerians, along with people from other African countries have accounted for a large proportion of non-European Union migrants to Ireland. John Paul II wrote "BEWARE OF CULTURES THAT COULD DESTROY YOUR CULTURE, RATHER EVANGELIZE IMMIGRANTS THROUGH YOUR CULTURE." He founded the Pontifical Council for Culture in 1982 with this in mind.

Now, how many of us have visited the Emerald Isle and kissed the stone in Blarney Castle, or made a pilgrimage to Our Lady of Knock? A famous Marian Shrine is Our Lady of Knock, Ireland. Our Lady, St. Joseph, and St. John the Evangelist appeared to 15 humble, hardworking Catholics of various ages in 1879. Since then, many pilgrims have experienced healings, and a Shrine was built. A brief word about Shrines, they must be sanctioned by the Church. Sensationalism, emotionalism, and the overly zealous can convince people of the veracity of an alleged apparition even though the Church has repudiated it or made no decision whatsoever. Anytime that Scripture or Sacred Tradition is contradicted, or anytime that disobedience to the pope is encouraged or dissent from the Magisterium (the teaching authority of the Church) or disrespect for the hierarchy, you can be sure that it's not an authentic apparition. Real apparitions occur to help boost but never to replace the Christian faith.

How many of us, no matter where we were, felt our eyes water as we listened to an Irish tenor (especially at twilight) sing these beautiful Irish songs that included words like the following:

> Just to hear again the ripple of the trout stream, the women in the meadows savin' hay, and to sit beside the turf-fire in the cabin, and see the sun go down on Galway Bay.

Over in Killarney many years ago, my mother sang a song to me in tones so sweet and low. Too-ra-loo-ra-loo-ra, too-ra-loo-ra-li.

> So they sprinkled it with stardust
> Just to make the shamrocks grow,
> And when they had it finished
> Shure they called it Ireland.

'Tis I'll be there in sunshine or in shadow, oh Danny boy, oh Danny boy, I love you so.

> I'll take you home again, Kathleen
> Across the ocean wild and wide.
> To where your heart has ever been.
> Since first you were my bonnie bride.

Mickey, pretty Mickey, with your hair of raven hue. In your smiling so beguiling, there's a bit of Killarney, bit of the blarney, can you blame anyone for falling in love with you.

Let us pray that all the people around the world, especially those with Irish roots, continue to pray that the Catholics in that beautiful Emerald Isle remain loyal to the teachings of the Catholic Church.

Erin Go Braugh
Bert Hoffman

ADDENDUM ONE TO IRELAND—A REVERIE

Roman Catholicism in Nineteenth-Century Great Britain, written by George P. Landow, Professor of English and Art History, Brown Universtiy.

The Roman Catholic church, which forms the largest body of Christians in the world, had a comparatively minor role in nineteenth-century England, Wales, and Scotland. Ever since Henry VIII founded the Church of England (or Anglican Church), the Catholic minority who had remained faithful to the Church of Rome often found themselves looked upon with suspicion and denied many civil rights, including that of serving in Parliament, owning certain kinds of property, and attending Oxford, Cambridge, and other major universities, which existed in large part to train Church of England Clergy.

Several nineteenth-century events markedly changed the position of British Catholics and their church. First, in 1829 Parliament granted them full civil rights, including the right to serve in the legislature. In 1840 Parliament followed this dramatic change in the condition and power of Roman Catholics by disestablishing—or removing the official tax-supported statues of—the Anglican Church in predominantly Catholic Ireland. The Oxford Movement, or Tractarianism, began as a reaction to what Keble, Newman, Pusey, and others believed was an illegal and unchristian interference by government in the affairs of God's Church. Ironically, it ended by defending many Catholic practices and rituals, such as elaborate ritual, confession, celibacy, and monastic orders, long rejected by British Protestants. As Newman and some of the other Tractarians attempted to distinguish Protestant from Catholic positions on the basis of church history and traditions, they found themselves drawn to the faith they had initially attacked and ended by converting to a religion many Britain considered subversive and fundamentally anti-British. When in 1850 Pope Pius IX reinstated the Roman Catholic church organization, including parishes and dioceses, many Protestants feared the worst, and their fears only increased when the Vatican Council of 1869-70 declared the Pope's pronouncements on morals and doctrine infallible, or incapable of error.

ADDENDUM TWO TO IRELAND—A REVERIE
Roman Catholic Church in Scotland

The Roman Catholic Church in Scotland describes the organization of worldwide Roman Catholic Church in the geographic area of Scotland, distinct from the Catholic Church in England & Wales and the Catholic Church in Ireland.

The term Roman Catholic is strictly inaccurate—this name was first applied by the English political and religious establishment, as the Church of England had royal patronage and thus there was a desire to describe catholicism as foreign. The Church of Scotland did not have royal patronage, so such a distinction was not made.

In the 2001 census about 16% of the population of Scotland described themselves as being Roman Catholic, compared with 42% claiming affiliation to the Church of Scotland.

One of the issues it has had to face is sectarianism, though this is now largely restricted to education and football in parts of the Central Belt, especially in the west, or to spillovers from Northern Ireland.

History

Christianity probably came to Scotland around the second century, and was firmly established by the sixth and seventh centuries. However, until the eleventh century, the relationship between the Church in Scotland and the Papacy is ambiguous. The Scottish 'Celtic' Church had marked liturgical and ecclesiological differences from the rest of Western Christendom. Some of these were resolved at the end of the seventh century following the Synod of Whitby and St. Columba's withdrawal to Iona, however, it was not until the ecclessiastical reforms of the eleventh century that the Scottish Church became an integral part of the Roman communion.

That remained the picture until the Reformation in the early sixteenth century, when the Church in Scotland broke with the papacy, and adopted a Calvinist confession. At that point the celebration of the Roman Mass was outlawed. When Mary Queen of Scots returned from France to rule, she found herself as a Roman Catholic in a largely Protestant state and Protestant court. However, some few thousand indigenous Scottish Roman Catholics remained mainly in a small strip from the north-east coast to the Western Isles. Significant strongholds included Moidart, Morar and Barra.

The Jacobit risings in 1715 and 1745 further damaged the Roman Catholic cause in Scotland and it was not until the start of Catholic Emancipation in 1793 that Romand Catholicism regained a civil respectability.

During the nineteenth century, Irish immigration substantially boosted the number of Scottish Roman Catholics (especially in the west), and by 1900 it was estimated the 90-95% were of full or partial Irish descent. A Roman Catholic hierarchy was re-introduced in the mid 19th century.

Organization

There are two archbishops and six bishops in Scotland:

* Archbishop of Saint Andrews and Edinburgh

  * Bishop of Aberdeen
  * Bishop of Argyll and the Isles
  * Bishop of Dunkeld
  * Bishop of Galloway

* Archbishop of Glasgow

  * Bishop of Motherwell
  * Bishop of Paisley

ADDENDUM THREE TO IRELAND—A REVERIE

Let us study three outstanding Irish Catholics, and let's start with who else but St. Patrick (March 17), apostle to Ireland (389-461). Robert Ellsberg in his book *All Saints* starts his biography which follows with this prayer of St. Patrick (he also wrote the biographies for the other two):

"Christ be with me,
Christ before me,
Christ behind me,
Christ in the heart of everyone who thinks of me,
Christ in the mouth of everyone who speaks of me,
Christ in every eye that sees me,
Christ in every ear that hears me."

Thanks to the Irish diaspora, the feast of St. Patrick is widely celebrated in many parts of the world. Admittedly, this celebration is more often an occasion for national pride than for reflection on the cause to which the saint dedicated his life. Ironically, St. Patrick is much better known for his apocryphal achievement—having rid the Emerald Isle of snakes—than for his actual accomplishments as a missionary. But even his great achievement, having established the Christian church in Ireland, tends to overshadow some of the more personal and poignant aspects of his life.

Patrick's mission to Ireland and its successful outcome is justly celebrated. But it is often forgotten that Patrick's first introduction to Ireland was involuntary. At the age of sixteen he was kidnapped by Irish raiders, stolen from his home, a village somewhere along the western coast of Roman Britain, and taken to Ireland as a slave. Previously he had lived relatively comfortable life as the son of a petty Roman official. This violent change in his life, as may well be supposed, was a shocking experience. He found himself sold to a local king who employed him in a variety of menial occupations, such as herding livestock on the desolate mountains of the north. As a slave, his life was not valued more highly than the beasts he tended. As he later wrote, "I was chastened exceedingly and humbled every day in hunger and nakedness."

At the same time, far from home and with little prospect of ever seeing his family again, he remembered who he was and where he came from. In particular, he clung fast to his faith as a Christian. Whereas previously he had been relatively indifferent in his faith, now he liked to spend his long days among the flocks reciting endlessly the prayers impressed on his memory since childhood. All the while he dreamed of escape. Eventually, after six years of captivity, an opportunity arose and he seized it. His flight involved a risky journey of two hundred miles to the sea, when he found a place on a boat sailing for the Continent. Thus, eventually after many further adventures, he made his way back to his home village.

The scene of his family reunion can scarcely be imagined. But the young man who had now returned from the dead was no longer the carefree adolescent of before. He bore the scars of a terrible ordeal, but also the zeal of a profound faith. In the light of this faith he was convinced that both his sufferings and his deliverance had been ordained for some divine purpose.

It was some years hence that this purpose became plain. While living in Gaul, where he had traveled to study for the priesthood, he had a series of dreams in which Irish voices, the voices of those who had stolen his youth, cried out to him, "We beseech thee to come and walk once more among us." At first his superiors resisted the idea of his return to Ireland, judging among other things that he lacked the learning and skills for such a dangerous mission. But he overcame their objections, and so in 432, by this time a consecrated bishop, he returned to the island from which providence had once aided his escape.

St. Patrick's thirty years as a wandering bishop in Ireland are wrapped in legend, but the scope of his achievements is a matter of historical record. Within ten years he had established the primatial see of Armagh and a network of churches and monasteries throughout the country, all in the hands of a native clergy. He personally baptized tens of thousands of the faithful and ordained hundreds of priests. Although he was not all alone in his work of evangelization, his stature as a patron of Ireland is well deserved.

But in a land that has been rent asunder by the memory of ancient crimes and injustices, it should be remembered that St. Patrick was himself the victim of Irish injustice before he ever became the symbol of Irish pride. His extraordinary return to the site of his oppression—not to wreak his vengeance, but to implant the reconciling seeds of his own hard-won faith—deserves appropriate commemoration. The gospel drove Patrick to return to his oppressors that he might devote his life to their peaceful conversion and the cause of their salvation. But the spiritual conquest of Ireland followed the prior victory of love over the anger and bitterness in his own heart. If the memory of this dimension of St. Patrick's life had long ago become a feature of his feast day celebration, it might be truly said that there are no serpents left in Ireland.

Our second outstanding Irish Catholic is St. Brigid of Ireland (February 1) Abbess of Kildare (c450-525)

> "I would like a great lake of beer for the King of the kings; I would like the people of heaven to be drinking it through time eternal."

Brigid lived in the era when traditional Irish religion was giving way to the formal institution of Christianity. The lives and legends of holy Brigid reflect that uneasy ebb and flow. It has been noted that in ancient times Brigid was, in fact, the name of the Celtic sun goddess. This has given rise to the suggestion that in St. Brigid, a nun and abbss of the fifth century, we find the repository of primeval religious memories and traditions. In any case, it seems that with the cult of St. Brigid (called "The Mary of the Gael") the Irish people maintained an image of the maternal face of God with which to complement the more patriarchal religion of St. Patrick and subsequent missionaries.

As best as can be discerned through the mists of legend, it is believed that Brigid was born into slavery and was later converted to Christianity by St. Patrick sometime in her childhood. She was granted her freedom when it proved impossible to curb her enthusiasm for giving alms; it seems she would otherwise have impoverished her master through such unauthorized largesse.

The themes of generosity and compassion are the feature of miracles without number. Brigid's only desire was "to satisfy the poor, to expel every hardship, to spare every miserable man." (That there remained any miserable souls in Ireland is hard to believe, given the extent of her recorded miracles.) Many of her marvels have a particularly maternal character, reflecting her propensity to nourish and give succor. Thus, "She supplied beer out of her one barrel to eighteen churches, which sufficed from Maundy Thursday to the end of the paschal time. Once a leprous woman asking for milk, there being none at hand she gave her cold water, but the water was turned into milk, and when she had drunk it the woman was healed."

Brigid became a nun and ultimately abbess of Kildare, which was a double monastery, consisting of both men and women. Through her fame as a spiritual teacher the Abbey of Kildare became a center for pilgrims. So great was the authority of Brigid, it seems that she even induced a bishop to join her community and to share her leadership. According to legend—which the church, for obvious reasons, has strenuously resisted—the bishop came to ordain Brigid as a fellow bishop.

Some chronicles cite this in a matter-of-fact way (it is, after all, scarcely less credible than many of the reports of Brigid's career). Others report the story while trying in some way to mitigate the scandal. It is suggested, for instance, that the bishop was so "intoxicated with the grace of God" that he didn't know what he was doing. Whatever the historical facts, the persistence of such a tale says a good deal about Brigid's status in the Irish conscience, and perhaps the effort to rectify the exclusion of such an extraordinary woman from the ranks of apostolic authority.

I selected Mollie Rogers as the third personality because her granparents came from Ireland to the United States, also her heroic life involved in some way all the nations we visited in our International Year. Let's read about these involvements.

Mollie Rogers (October 9)
Foundress of the Maryknoll Sisters (1882-1955)

"There is nothing more astonishing that life, just as it is, nothing more miraculous than growth and change and development, just as revealed to us. And as happens so often when we stop to regard God's work, there is nothing to do but wonder and thank Him, realizing how little we planned, how little we achieved, and yet how much has been done."

Mollie Rogers dated the beginning of her vocation to a summer evening at Smith College when a crowd of her fellow students rushed outdoors singing "Onward Christian Soldiers." They had just signed the Student Volunteer pledge to go to China as Protestant missionaries. Mollie shared their exhilaration, mixed with a certain regret that there was no similar Catholic mission group that she could support. She made her way to the parish church and there, "before Jesus in the tabernacle, I measured my faith and the expression of it by the sight I had just witnessed. From that moment I had work to do, little or great, God alone knew."

There was no immediate issue from this resolution. But several years later in 1905 Mollie, now an instructor at Smith, sought out Father James Anthony Walsh, local director of the Society for the Propagation of the Faith in Boston. He immediately enlisted her help with Field Afar, a new journal aimed at stimulating mission awareness in the U.S. Church.

Walsh, an Irish-American priest in his thirties, was at the time collaborating with Father Thomas Price from North Carolina on a plan to establish an American foreign mission society. Their objective: the great expanse of China. It is hard today to appreciate the magnitude of this vision. Until 1908 the United States was itself designated as a mission territory. America was still in the midst of a massive influx of European immigrants, and a good number of the Catholic priests serving in the country were themselves foreign born. Overseas mission at the time was considered a protestant enterprise, while the Catholic church had its hands full dealing with more pressing needs at home. Nevertheless in 1911 Walsh and Price won support from the American bishops to establish a mission seminary. This was the origin of the Catholic Foreign Mission Society of America, soon to be known as Maryknoll.

Mollie was one of a small group of women who volunteered to join the priests in Ossining, New York, to help with the launching of this project. Their work was mostly confined to secretarial work on Field Afar. But as the Society took shape Mollie became more and more convinced that the women had a wider role to play than as mere helpers to the priests. Why, she asked, shouldn't women also serve as overseas missionaries? She won over Walsh and Price to her project. They perceived the advantage of women missioners who could more easily relate to the women of China. But to pursue this plan it was necessary that they form a religious congregation.

Mollie had felt no special call to become a nun, but if that is what it took to become a missioner she was game.

This plan encountered resistance from Vatican officials who doubted that women were suited to the rugged demands of mission. The congregation that Rogers envisioned also represented a departure from the conventional model of religious life. She wished her Sisters to live amid the people—not cooped up in monastic enclosures, but able to move freely about to bear witness to the gospel. Despite reservations, the Vatican in 1920 granted approval. A year later Mollie Rogers and twenty-one other women made their formal religious vows as Maryknoll Sisters of St. Dominic.

The Sisters were helped in their early formation by members of other religious congregations. But Mollie Rogers, or Mother Mary Joseph as she was known, found it difficult to adjust to the discipline and spirituality of these nuns, rooted in the traditions of the old world. Rogers was interested instead in adapting religious life to the needs of mission. Refusing "to be hampered by an over-regimented and parceled-out prayer life," she fought hard to impress on the congregation the importance of flexibility and individuality. Describing the ideal Maryknoll Sister, she said,

> I would have her distinguished by Christ-like charity, a limpid simplicity of soul, heroic generosity, selflessness, unfailing loyalty, prudent zeal, gracious courtesy, an adaptable disposition, solid piety, and the saving grace of a kindly humor.

The first mission of the Maryknoll Sisters was among Japanese immigrants on the West Coast. But soon Roger's dream was fulfilled when the first Maryknoll Sisters were sent to China. Again, as she had hoped, the Sisters branched out beyond the work of support for the priests or traditional works of charity. In China, and eventually elsewhere, Maryknoll Sisters went out into the countryside to befriend the poor and to engage in the direct work of evangelization. Other missions followed in Korea, the Philippines, and eventually throughout the world.

Rogers followed the work of her Sisters with maternal pride and made several trips overseas to survey their progress. But it was not her vocation to join them. Instead she remained at the mother-house directing the congregation until she retired from office in 1950. At the time of her death on October 9, 1955, there were eleven hundred Maryknoll Sisters serving worldwide.

In years to come the Maryknoll Sisters would achieve a heroic image for their exploits in the jungles of Africa and Latin America, and for their sufferings during World War II and under Communist persecution in China. Later still, beginning in the 1960's, their commitment to social justice and their "option for the poor" would entail a different type of heroism. But as the congregation grew and evolved over time the Sisters continued to draw inspiration from the vision and personality of Mollie Rogers, who once wrote, "Love, work, prayer, and suffering will sustain us in the future as they have in the past. All who are here now, all who will come after us, will have no other tools than these with which to build."

FRANCE—A REVERIE BON JOUR

The Church of France is part of the worldwide Roman Catholic Church, under the spiritual leadership of the Pope and curia in Rome. There are an estimated 15 million baptized Catholics in France (77% of the population, in 98 dioceses, served by 23,000 priests). However, according to a 2003 poll, the numbers of believing and practicing Catholics are much lower. According to FROESE (2001), 54% of the French are atheist or agnostic.

Let us see what happens when EVIL slowly creeps into the lives of the citizens and the government of any nation. During the middle of the 18th century, lukewarm attitudes became evident in the French Church. Religious practices and morals were in decline. Then came the view that the Church wasn't necessary and that the human mind didn't need any guidance from divine grace. Reason alone was sufficient and faith was nonsensical. This way of thinking was called rationalism. Philosophy and empirical science sought truths that the human mind could attain. Theology wasn't treated as a science but as a superstition. The rationalists saw religion as a myth. And they had no respect for divine revelation. The end of the 18th century witnessed the dawn of both the American and French Revolutions. We know the lofty Christian ideals of our founding fathers as set forth in our Declaration of Independence and in our Constitution; thanks be to GOD! Let's briefly look at the non-Christian goals of the French Revolution in 1789.

In that year (1789), the atmosphere began to change in France. Church land was taken over by the government with the understanding that the state would take care of the clergy. The following year all monasteries and convents were suppressed, one-third of the dioceses were done away with. In 1793, the Reign of Terror began, resulting in the execution of many, often innocent, people. King Louis XVI was deposed and put to death. Hatred for the Church reached the point of insanity. Marie Antoinette and many loyal Catholics met death at the guillotine, very common in France during this time. The Cathedral of Notre Dame in Paris, a bastion of French Catholicism, was reduced to a barracks for animals, and a statue of the goddess of reason replaced the one of the Virgin Mary. Napoleon eventually came to power in France and tried to swoon the

French people knowing they were still basically Catholic at heart by making pseudo and bogus overtures to the Catholic Church. In 1801, he signed a concordat (Vatican treaty) with Pope Pius VII giving back church property seized during the French Revolution and the infamous Reign of Terror. He went so far as to have the Pope come to Paris and crown him emperor in the Cathedral of Notre Dame. With audacious pride, he grabbed the crown from the aged pope and literally crowned himself and then his Empress Josephine.

Sadly, the Revolution drastically changed Catholicism forever—not only in France but also throughout Europe. The people of France were able to declare themselves non-Catholic or non-Christian. By the creation of a civil state, divorce became acceptable. Anti-clericalism and atheism later flourished in a country that once was called the Eldest Daughter of the Church. How sad!

Here are a few more comments to finish off this phase of French history. After an unsuccessful campaign in Russia, Napoleon was defeated in 1814 and exiled to Elba. He returned to Paris a year later (1815) for a short reign of 100 days until his defeat by the British Duke of Wellington in the battle of Waterloo in Belgium. He was exiled to the island of St. Helena until his death from cancer in 1821. After Napoleon's defeat and exile, two factions occupied France. The Liberals wanted to perpetuate the ideals of the French Revolution. The Conservatives wanted a restoration of the monarchy and Catholicism. However, the Catholic Church in France never fully recovered from the devastation that the Revolution created. Seeds of indifference to the true faith were sewn and they blossomed and flourished into the 20th Century after World War II.

Before ending this reverie, we should thank France for giving us that magnificent and inspiring Statue of Liberty which greeted so many of our grandparents as they immigrated to these United States of America. The statue was unveiled on October 28, 1886 on Bedloe's Island in New York Harbor. This huge work of art and engineering was a gift from the people of France to the people of the United States in commemoration of the Alliance of 1778 between the two nations. On its base was inscribed these words:

> Give me you're tired, you're poor, Your huddled masses yearning to breathe free, the wretched refuse of your teeming shore, send these, the homeless, tempest—tossed to me: I lift my lamp beside the golden door.

We can also thank France for another great gift they gave us but in an indirect way. The World's Fair of 1889 was held in Paris. The chief exhibit of the fair was the Eiffel Tower. Daniel Burnham, in charge of the World's Fair of 1893 to be held in Chicago, issued a challenge to American engineers to create something to outdo the Eiffel Tower. Many entries were submitted but the winning entry was submitted by a thirty-four-year-old bridge engineer from

Pittsburg named George Washington Gale Ferris. His Ferris Wheel was both new and audacious. It became the chief exhibit and landmark of the fair. His big steel wheel on the Midway Plaisance, the exposition's commercially run entertainment strip, was the fair's only rival in popular appeal of the nighttime illumination and a foretaste of how technology would usher in a new industry of mass entertainment. Merci Beaucoup, France (thank you very much, France)!

"If today you hear His voice, harden not your heart"

Ce La Vie, No! Ce La Guerre!
(That's life, no! That's war!)
Au Revoir,
Bert Hoffman

ADDENDUM ONE TO FRANCE—A REVERIE

No Catholic Reverie on France would be complete without mentioning two of her most famous and courageous citizens, St. Joan of Arc and St. John Vianney, the Cure of Ars. These brief biographies were obtained from All Saints by Robert Ellsberg and from Saint of the Day by Leonard Foley, O.F.M., and Pat McCloskey, O.F.M.

St. Joan of Arc
Maid of Orleans (1412?-1431)

"On being asked whether she did not believe that she was subject to the church which is on earth, namely, our Holy Father the Pope, cardinals, archbishops, bishops, and prelates of the church, she replied: Yes, but our Lord must be served first."

Joan of Arc is one of the most attractive and intriguing heroes of history. Her life has been the subject of countless studies, as well as the inspiration for films, plays, novels, and poems. She has been claimed, variously, as a symbol of patriotism, military valor, and feminism, and as a martyr of conscience. At least since 1920, when she was formally canonized, she has also been claimed as a Christian saint. Just what kind of a saint remains the subject of debate. But among canonized saints she enjoys what is probably the unique distinction of having been previously condemned by the church and executed as a heretic. She thus may be legitimately claimed not only as a patron of France, but of all those holy men and women who have been vilified in their own time in the hope of eventual vindication.

Her familiar story remains compelling. As a young peasant girl in southern France, she claimed to hear the voices of the Archangel Michael, later joined by *St. Catherine of Alexandria and St. Margaret, charging her with a mission to save France by restoring the Dauphin to his rightful throne and driving the English enemy from French soil. It was partly a reflection of the desperate times that she managed to convince the Dauphin and his advisors to put her in command of his faltering army. She turned the tide of the war by successfully breaking the English siege on Orleans. Dressed in soldier's attire and brandishing the standard, she inspired the French troops to valor and managed a string of military victories which paved the way for the crowning of the Dauphin as Charles VII, King of France.

But from this pinnacle the wheel of fortune quickly turned. In a subsequent battle she was captured by Burgundian troops who sold her to their English allies. She was imprisoned for a year and subjected to an interminable interrogation by an ecclesiastical court sympathetic to the English cause. Though her fate was never in doubt, the court sought desperately to discredit her by finding evidence of heresy or witchcraft. Joan deflected their questions with guileless wit and impressed many with her evident faith and purity of heart. Throughout she held adamantly to the authority of her "voices," and she would not give up her male clothing. These were the bases on which she was eventually convicted.

On May 30, 1431, Joan was publicly burned at the stake. Her ashes were thrown in the Seine. She was nineteen years old.

In 1455 an official ecclesiastical investigation examined Joan's court proceedings and found her innocent of the charges against her. She was canonized 450 years later, a testimony to the longstanding interest in her cause. Even then, however, there was a certain vagueness about the kind of holiness she represented. Not wanting to call her a martyr, the church emphasized instead her piety and virginity.

There is no gainsaying Joan's purity and ardent faith. This accounts in part for the perennial fascination with her story; she epitomizes the confrontation between purity and the corruptions of power. But unlike traditional saints, she employed her piety not so much in the service of the church but in the cause of national liberation. She represents a kind of political holiness, not a "church" piety or the mystical rapture of the convent, but a mysticism expressed in commitment to the world and engagement in the events of history. In this, she was more like the Maccabean martyrs of Israel than her virginal patrons Sts. Catherine and Margaret. It is useless to speculate what supposed interest these saints might have had in the dynastic fortunes of France. But for us that is not the issue; Joan's "voices" spoke to her alone, and what is important is the courage of her response. Thus she inspires us to attend to the voices of our own angels and to respond with equal faith.

An illiterate peasant girl, a shepherd, a "nobody," she heeded a religious call to save her country when all the "somebodies" of her time proved unable or unwilling to meet the challenge. She stood up before princes of the church and state and the most learned authorities of her world and refused to compromise her conscience or deny her special vocation. She paid the ultimate price for her stand. And in doing so she won a prize far more valuable than the gratitude of the Dauphin or the keys of Orleans.

St. John Vianney
Cure of Ars (1786-1859)

"To be a saint one must be beside oneself, one must lose one's head."

The early life of John Vianney contained no foreshadowing of greatness in any field. He was born to a peasant family in a village near Lyons. Though he desired nothing else but to be a priest, his humble background and lack of education made it unlikely that he could ever realize such a vocation. Nevertheless with the help of private tutoring he secured a place in a seminary. His studies were interrupted when he was conscripted to serve in the army. On his way to a posting in Spain he deserted and went into hiding for several years in a neighboring village. Only with an amnesty in 1810 was he able to resume his formation.

For all his zeal, Vianney proved to be a miserable student. It was only with grave reservations that he was recommended for ordination. In the end, however, his evident piety and goodness won the day. As one of his sponsors noted, "The Church wants not only learned priests but even more holy ones." Thus he was finally ordained at the age of twenty-nine. He served for a brief time as curate in his home parish. And then in 1817 he was named the parish priest of Ars-en-Dombes, a village of 250 souls, as remote and insignificant a place as his bishop could find.

To Vianney there was nothing insignificant about his new home. The size of the village was unimportant. He regarded himself as answerable for the salvation of his flock. This was an awesome charge, which he accepted with all the determination of a soldier ordered to hold his position. Compensating for lack of learning, he girded himself for his responsibilities by ascetic zeal. This did not go unnoticed. It was said that the new cure lived on nothing but potatoes. He never seemed to sleep. When not visiting parishioners or performing the sacraments he could invariably be found in the church, fixed in silent adoration of the Eucharist.

The cure's sermons were simple and unsophisticated. His theology was rudimentary. His efforts to elevate the spiritual level of his community by combating the evils of profanity, public dances, and work on Sunday seemed, even at the time, to verge on the naïve. But what gradually dawned on his parishioners and began to work its gradual effect was the consciousness that their souls mattered to this holy priest and that he suffered for their sins.

For all his simplicity, there was one area in which Vianney acquired a reputation for genius: his extraordinary gifts as a confessor. It was said that he had an ability to read souls. With disarming simplicity, the Cure D'Ars was apparently able to discern the secrets of his penitents, and unlock the barriers that prevented them from knowing and loving God. This gift attracted a growing stream of penitents which gradually expanded so as to lay claim to nearly all of his waking hours. Fixed in his cramped confessional, shivering in the winter, stifling in the summer, he would sit ten, twelve, as many as eighteen hours a day.

Toward the end of his life the railroad provided special trains to accommodate the heavy traffic of pilgrims to the famous confessional in Ars. By the time of his death in 1859 Vianney was one of the most beloved figures in France. Various honors were bestowed on him. Napoleon III, in a curious gesture, sent him the medal of the Legion of Honor. Vianney refused to take it out of the box, remarking, "I don't know what I have done to deserve this except to be a deserter."

Certainly Vianney never sought or anticipated such fame. It was literally one more cross that he shouldered. Vianney could not imagine any more important calling than to serve as the parish priest of the village of Ars. This was the post where he had been placed to care for the souls of his flock, ready, like the good shepherd, to lay down his life for them, if that were required.

St. John Vianney was canonized in 1925 by pope Pius XI. At the same time he was named patron saint of all parish priests.

As pastor of the parish at Ars, John encountered people who were indifferent and quite comfortable with their style of living. His vision led them through severe fasts and short nights of sleep. (Some devils can only be cast out by prayer and fasting.)

With Catherine Lassagne and Benedicta Lardet, he established La Providence, a home for girls. Only a man of vision could have such trust that God would provide for the spiritual and material needs of all those who came to make La Providence their home. Who, but a man with vision, could keep going with ever-increasing strength?

Indifference toward religion, coupled with a love for material comfort, seem to be common signs of our times. A person from another planet observing us would not likely judge us to be pilgrim people, on our way to somewhere else. John Vianney, on the other hand, was a man on a journey with his goal before him at all times.

Recommending liturgical prayer, John Vianney would say, "Private prayer is like straw scattered here and there: If you set it on fire it makes a lot of little flames. But gather these straws into a bundle and light them, and you get a mighty fire, rising like a column into the sky; public prayer is like that."

May we follow his advice to "Open your heart so the word of God may enter it, take root in it, and bear fruit there for eternal life."

ADDENDUM TWO—FRANCE—A REVERIE

I would be open to criticism if I did not mention two of her most modern popular Catholic saints; and a brief biography of each: St. Bernadette Soubirous (1844-1879) and St Therese of Lisieux (1873-1897). These biographies were obtained from Catholicism for Dummies by Reverend John Trigilio, Jr., PHD, THD and Reverend Kenneth Brighenti, PHD.

St. BERNADETTE SOUBIROUS

Bernadette was born on January 7, 1844, in Lourdes, France. Her parents, Francis and Louis Soubirous, were extremely poor but loved their daughter very much. She suffered from severe asthma, which kept her behind a few years in school.

The faithful believe that on February 11, 1858, she saw an apparition of Mary in a cave on the banks of the Gave River near Lourdes. The woman didn't identify herself but asked Bernadette to faithfully come to the grotto as it was called and to pray the Rosary for the conversion of sinners so that they might turn away from their evil ways and come back to God.

Initially, the townsfolk thought she was insane. But on February 25, the woman asked Bernadette to dig in the soil until a spring of water would appear. She did as the woman asked, and the spring did appear.

It's believed that the water had immediate miraculous properties, and the skeptic populace of Lourdes flocked to the grotto to get some of this healing water. The blind could see, the lame could walk, the deaf could hear, the sick regained their health, and so on.

The faithful believe that on March 25, 1858, the woman announced to Bernadette that she was the Immaculate Conception. Ironically, the dogma of the Immaculate Conception had only been defined by Pope Pius IX four earlier (1854), and scholars maintain that an intellectually challenged peasant girl from the rinky-dink town of Lourdes couldn't have heard about such a term let alone understand it.

The public authorities, which were anti-Catholic and anti-clerical, closed the grotto only to have the Emperor Louis Napoleon III order it reopened. His son had taken ill and his wife, the Empress Eugenie of France, obtained some Lourdes water, which the faithful believe cured his imperial royal highness.

Bernadette didn't live a normal life after that, and in 1866 she entered the convent of the Sisters of Notre Dame in Nevers where she spent the rest of her short life. Thirteen years later, she was found to have an illness similar to tuberculosis, which produced excruciating and chronic pain, but she said the healing waters of Lourdes were not for her. She died in 1879, but today, her body remains incorrupt (free of decay despite the lack of embalming or mummification treatments). The Shrine at Lourdes is an international place of prayer, and some miraculous healings are still being attributed to those waters from the grotto where Catholics believe Mary appeared to Bernadette.

THERESE OF LISIEUX

Francoise-Marie Therese, the youngest of the five daughters, was born on January 2, 1873. At the age of four, her mother died and left her father with five girls to raise on his own. The eldest, 13-year-old Marie helped much. The second oldest, Pauline, later joined the Carmelite order of nuns and was then followed by her sister Marie. Therese wanted to join her sisters as a Carmelite when she was but 14 years old. The order normally made the girls wait until they were 16 before entering the convent or monastery, but Therese was adamant. She accompanied her father to a general papal audience of His Holiness Pope Leo XIII and surprised everyone by throwing herself before the pontiff, begging to become a Carmelite. The wise pope replied, "If the good God wills, you will enter." When she returned home, the local bishop allowed her to enter early. On April 9, 1888, at the age of 15, Therese entered the Carmelite monastery of Lisieux and joined her two sisters.

On September 8, 1890, she took her final vows. She showed remarkable spiritual insights for someone so young, but it was due to her childlike (not childish) relationship with Jesus. Her superiors asked her to keep memoirs of her thoughts and experiences.

In 1896, at the age of 23, she coughed up blood and was diagnosed with tuberculosis. She lived only one more year, and it was a long year in which she endured intense, painful, and bitter physical suffering. Yet it's said that she did so lovingly, to join Jesus Christ on the cross. She offered up her pain and suffering for souls that might be lost, so they could come back to God. Her little way consisted of, in her own words, of "doing little things often, doing them well, and doing them with love." She died on September 30, 1897.

Despite the fact that she lived such a short and cloistered life, having never left her monastery let alone her native France, she was later named patroness of the Foreign Missions. The reason was that during World War I, many soldiers who were wounded in battle and recuperating in hospitals—as well as those who were in the trenches awaiting their possible death—read her autobiography, and it changed their hearts. Many who had grown cold or lukewarm in their Catholic faith wanted to imitate St. Therese of Lisieux, who was also known as the Little Flower, and become a little child of God.

And I would be equally remiss if I did not at least briefly mention St. Margaret Mary Alacoque, Virgin (1647-1690). Born in Burgundy, France, she entered the Visitation convent at Paray-le-Monial (1671). Between 1673 and 1676 she experienced four visions in which Christ revealed His love and mercy for all humanity and was told to record them by her confessor, Jesuit Fr. Claude la Colombiere. At first these revelations provoked resistance and rejection from her community, but by 1686 the community too was honoring the heart of Jesus, and in 1688, a chapel in the garden was consecrated to the Sacred Heart (1688). Two years later Margaret died, but the devotion she had begun at Paray was now firmly established. Like her, may we understand that "one cannot better show one's love for Christ than by loving one's neighbor for love of Him."

MEXICO—A REVERIE

Ah, gentle reader, somewhere long ago we heard and were taught the meaning of the word CULTURE and that the culture of a person consisted of his/her heredity and environment. Unbelievably, Webster sort of agrees in his definition of culture as (1.) a particular stage of advancement in civilization or the characteristic features of such a stage or state, and (2.) act of developing by education, discipline, training, etc. So, any nation has a national culture if all its citizens, or mostly all, have shared the same heredity and environment. Obviously the United States does not have a national culture but Mexico has!! So to better understand our good and God-fearing neighbors to the South and most especially to understand the very many good and hard-working Mexican people that now live in our country, let us learn more about their experiences and history that helped shape their culture by looking at four time periods in their history:

1. 1531—The Apparition of Mary to St. Juan Diego
   (Mexico eventually become a Catholic nation)
2. 1820 to the 1850's
   (Annexation of Texas and the Mexican Cession)
3. 1876 to 1926
   (Relations between Mexico and the Catholic Church)
4. 1926 to the present time
   (Mexico invaded by different 'isms')

Remember every person has a culture, nations that have a national culture are becoming fewer and fewer. Both Popes, John Paul II and Benedict XVI, talk about two world cultures, the culture of life and the culture of death. Both Popes have written that the world is in its final confrontation between good and evil. But neither Pope mentions a time table. Now, with that cheerful thought, read on!

The Basilica of Guadalupe contains the miraculous image of Our Lady of Guadalupe that was imprinted by Mary on the cloak of an Aztec Indian, 57 year-old St. Juan Diego, on December 12, 1531, note, this is only THIRTY-NINE years after Columbus discovered America!

Walking north of Mexico City in the Tepayac hill country, Juan Diego saw the Virgin Mary, but she had the appearance of an Aztec woman, not an European, and she was pregnant. She directed Juan Diego to go to the local bishop and tell him that she wanted a church built in her honor. After waiting several hours to see the Spanish-born aristocratic Bishop Fray Juan de Zumarraga, Juan Diego was granted an audience. The respectful yet incredulous Bishop told Juan Diego that he needed a sign from heaven that this was indeed God's will to build a church in that location. Juan Diego told Mary what the bishop had requested, and she told him to gather roses from a bush that appeared out of nowhere. These Castilian roses weren't indigenous to Mexico, and certainly not in cold December, but they were popular in Spain. It just so happened that the bishop's hobby was gardening, and he'd been an official rose expert in Spain before being sent to Mexico. Juan Diego carried the roses in his TILMA (cloak) to the bishop, opened his garment, and the bishop fell to his knees. Not only were the roses beautiful and rare, but also, a gorgeous image of Our Lady of Guadalupe was on the tilma. She was like the scriptural passage that describes a woman who is "clothed with the sun and upon her head a crown of twelve stars with the moon under her feet and she was with child" (Revelation 12:1-12). To this day, science can't explain how that image got onto the tilma. It's not painted, dyed, sewn, printed, sealed, or the product of any man=made process, nor is it a natural phenomenon. It remains on display in the Basilica Church in Mexico where Pope John Paul II canonized Juan Diego in 2002. Millions of people from South, Central and North America, Europe, Africa and Asia visit this holy place.

The second time period we should look at to help understand the history and culture of Mexico would be the 1820's-1850's. By the 1840's Americans had again become expansion-minded. They believed that their country was destined to spread to the Pacific Coast, or perhaps over the entire North American Continent, a belief known as 'manifest destiny'. Manifest destiny was promoted by (1.) land-hungry Americans who eyed tracts of rich but sparsely settled lands, (2.) patriots who feared British designs upon such lands, (3.) Eastern merchants whose ships trading with Asia needed ports on the Pacific coast, (4.) democratic-minded people who believed that American territorial growth meant the spreading of freedom, and (5.) nationalists who sought American greatness.

Americans were invited by newly independent Mexico in 1821 to settle in her northern province of Texas. Stephen Austin led the first group of land-hungry Americans, others soon followed. By 1830 some 20,000 whites with 1000 Negro slaves had come to Texas from the United States. In the 1830's friction developed between the Mexican government and the American settlers, as Mexico attempted to (a.) halt further American immigration into Texas, (b) free the Negro slaves, and (c) deprive Texas of local self-government. Texas Revolution took place in 1836. Claiming a parallel with the American Revolution against Britain, the Texans rebelled for independence. At the ALAMO, a fortified church mission at San Antonio, a Texas force was besieged and overwhelmed by a Mexican army under General SANTA ANNA. The bloody massacre of the Alamo defenders further inflamed the Texans, whose battle cry became "Remember the Alamo!" Led by Sam Houston, the Texans won a great victory at the Battle of San Jacinto, capturing Santa Anna and driving his troops out of Texas. The settlers proclaimed the Republic of Texas (the Lone Star Republic), elected Sam Houston as President, and requested annexation by the United States. While Southerners favored the annexation of Texas, Northeasterners opposed it. Northeasterners feared (a.) the extension of slave territory, (b.) increased Southern membership in the House of Representatives, and (c.) the possible division of Texas into several states, which would greatly increase Southern membership in the Senate. In 1844 Northern opposition and fear of war with Mexico led the Senate to defeat an annexation treaty. But in 1845, just before POLK took office, President Tyler suggested that Congress admit Texas to the Union by means of a joint resolution. Whereas a treaty requires a two-thirds vote in the Senate, a joint resolution requires only a majority vote, but in each house. The resolution was approved, and Texas joined the Union.

We went to war with Mexico in the years 1846-1848. These were the causes of that war. Mexican patriots resented (a.) the American annexation of Texas, (b.) our claim that the southern boundary of Texas was the Rio Grande, rather than the Nueces River, and (c.) the ambition of American expansionists to acquire additional Mexican Territory. In addition, the Mexican government owed money to a number of American Citizens. The unstable Mexican government, in response to public opinion, refused to receive the American negotiator John Slidell. The Mexicans refused to listen to Slidell's proposals that the United States purchase their New Mexico and California territories for as much as $30 million and assume Mexico's debts to Americans in exchange for the Rio Grande boundary. Instead Mexican and United States troops entered the disputed area between the Rio Grande and the Nuecees River, and in 1846 a minor clash took place. President Polk, infuriated, informed Congress that "Mexico has invaded our territory and shed American blood upon American soil." Polk requested and secured a declaration of war. Although most Northeastern congressmen voted for the declaration, many Northeasterners condemned the war as an imperialist plot against a weak neighbor to seize land and extend slavery. Most Southerners and Westerners enthusiastically welcomed the war. American volunteer armies soon demonstrated their military superiority. General Zachary Taylor ("Old Rough and Ready") won victory after victory in northern Mexico. General Winfield Scott captured VERA CRUZ and Mexico City, the capital.

Colonel Stephen Kearny occupied New Mexico and advanced on California. In California, Captain John C. Fremont led American settlers to drive out the Mexican authorities and establish the temporary California (Bear Flag) Republic. Mexico's defeat was complete. By the Treaty of Guadalupe Hidalgo in 1848, Mexico (a) accepted the Rio Grande as the southern boundary of Texas, and (b) gave up California and the province of New Mexico, together called the MEXICAN CESSION. This area was eventually carved up into five states and parts of two others. The United States agreed to pay Mexico $15 million and to assume the claims of American citizens against the Mexican government. Five years after purchasing the Mexican Cession for $15 million, the United States paid Mexico $10 million for a small strip of land in southern Arizona and New Mexico. This land, called the GADSDEN PURCHASE, provided a favorable railroad route into California. Many Americans felt, however, that the large sum paid for this territory was "CONSCIENCE MONEY." By the way, Father Hidalgo, S.J. died in front of a firing squad.

Let us now turn to the third period of Mexican history. During the period from 1876 to 1916 relations between the Catholic Church and the Mexican government were stable. The Catholic Church intended on having steady relations since they wanted to increase their political hold in Mexico. PORFIRIO DIAZ was obsessed and worried about the American expansionist threat. Porfiro Diaz has been quoted as saying:

> "Persecution of the Church, whether or not the clergy enter into the matter, means war, and such a war that the Government can win if the war is only against its own people, through the humiliating, despite costly and dangerous support of the United States. Without its religion, Mexico is irretrievably lost." Diaz strengthened the Mexican government ties with the Catholic Church with an agreement formulated in 1905. The church's influence over Mexico transcended due to the amount of changes that occurred while Diaz was in power. These institutional reforms included: administrative, reorganization, improved training of the laity, the expansion of the Catholic press, an expansion of Catholic education, and the growth of the Church's influence in rural areas. The lack of enforcement of anti-clerical laws by Diaz can also be attributed to the profound influence of his wife who was a devout Catholic. After Francisco Madero's victory over Porfirio Diaz, (the early stages of the Mexican Revolution), Madero continued to have close ties with the Catholic Church. However, this changed since Madero was a weak leader. VICTORIANO HUIRTA eventually overthrew MADERO in a bloody coud'etat in 1911. As the Mexican Revolution progressed, the Constitutionist of VENUSTIANO CARRANZA denounced clerical involvement in Mexican governmental affairs. They protested that they

were not persecuting the Catholic religion but wanted to reduce the Church's political influence. The Constitutionalists did not at first take any formal action. ALVARO OBREGON and the Constitutionalists eventually took active measures to reduce the profound influence of the Catholic Church. On May 19, 1914, OBREGON'S forces sentenced Bishop ANDRES SEGURA and other clerical officials to jail for eight years because of their participation in a revolt. While Obregon was in control of Mexico City during February 1915, he ordered the Church to pay 500,000 pesos to alleviate the suffering of poor Mexicans. VENUSTIANO CARRANZA assumed the presidency on May 1, 1915. Carranza and his followers felt that the clergy were turning people against him by spreading propaganda. Soon after, Carranza took total control of Mexico and developed a new Constitution with the intention of diminishing the Church's political sway and power within Mexico. Anti-clerical elements were included in the 1917 Mexican Constitution. Five elements in the Constitution were aimed at reducing the Catholic Church's influence in Mexican domestic affairs. Article 3 enforced secular education in Mexican schools. Monastic vows and orders were outlawed in Article 5. Article 24 prevented public worship outside the confines of the Church buildings. According to article 27, religious institutions were denied the right to acquire, hold, or administer real property. Furthermore, all real estate held by religious institutions through third parties like hospitals, schools, was declared national property. Finally in article 130, it declared all basic civil responsibilities like voting or commenting on public affairs was taken away from Church officials. The Mexican government was extremely harsh in their attempt to eliminate the Catholic church's legal existence in Mexico. The stern premises of the 1917 Constitution sttributed to the rise of resentment between the church and state. For eight years after these provisions were instituted, they were not rigorously enforced by the Mexican government. This changed in 1926 when PLUTARCO ELIAS CALLES reinforced laws to decrease clerical power. In June 1926, Calles recognized a decree often referred to as "Calles Law." Under the provision, Article 130 of the 1917 Mexican Constitution was re-established. Church officials were upset by the suddenness of Calles' decision. The regulation which annoyed the Catholic Church was Article 19, which decreed the compulsory registration of the clergy, for it allowed the government to hand over churches." The Catholic Church took a stand against the Mexican government. The internal political dissension became a concern for all Mexicans since the regulations by Calles reduced the Catholic Church's influence. The disagreement turned violent. When over five thousand Cristeros initiated an armed rebellion, the Mexican government and the Catholic Church engaged in bloody battle which lasted for a three-year period.

The fourth time period is 1926 to the present. The 20th century ushered in the isms: TOTALITARIANISM, COMMUNISM, FACISM, NAZISM, RELATISM, SECULAR HUMANISM, MATERIALISM, just to mention a few that operated not only in Mexico but in many nations of the world. In all the isms, religion is only tolerated if it does not conflict in any way with the "ism party" ideology. Since the Gospels do conflict with party thought, Christian religion is often suppressed. These forces of evil recognize that the Catholic Church is the strongest force for good. Therefore they do everything in their power to destroy it, such as: destroying churches but allowing people to worship in the churches that remained but they could not be instructed in the faith, nor could they gather for prayer or discussions; religious ceremonies were replaced by civil ones, oppressive measures were used to discredit religious groups, they tried to suppress the activities of Catholic action groups; many evil governments actively persecuted the church: church property was nationalized, education was thoroughly secularized, religious orders were suppressed and disbanded, in some places extremists burned churches and attacked and, in some cases, killed priests and religious; some isms methodically destroyed all church organizations and clamped down on the Catholic press. In expressing confused ideas, the 'isms' have great subtlety and sympathy. It is in expressing clear ideas that they generally find their limitations. This is how the forces of evil operate. Unfortunately, as you read, Mexico did not escape some of these attacks. Let us not forget the hundreds and hundreds of Mexican martyrs of the 20th century. Let us now look at the end of the 20th century. The Catholic Church is the world's largest Christian church, and its largest religious grouping. The 2000 census reported that Mexico had some 75 million Catholics among the population aged five years old and above, which equates to around 88% of the total population. Today, Mexico is divided into 88 Dioceses with 13,700 priests and 36,000 men and women in religious orders.

So, my gentle RRC readers, it might be very interesting to browse through Mexican History books covering these four time periods to better understand the feeling and culture of the Mexican people. Now let us conclude our reverie with these prayers

"Mary, Patroness of the Americas, pray for us."
"Mary, Mediatrix of all graces
Please protect and guide Mexico,
And send them vocations.
This we pray!"

"O Mary, Seat of Wisdom, pray for us."
> "O Mary, our Lady of Guadalupe,
> Send us that spiritual wisdom, so that
> We, the church militant, can be
> Victorious in our continuous battle against
> The forces of evil—This we pray!"

"VIVA CRISTO REY", these were the last words of Padre Miquel Pro, S.J. who suffered and died for his faith. He was beatified by John Paul II in 1988.

Bert Hoffman

ADDENDUM ONE TO MEXICO—A REVERIE

The most important event in the history of Mexico was the appearance of The Blessed Virgin Mary to Juan Diego on December 9, 1531. December 9th is now the feast day of Blessed Juan Diego. I have again gone to my friend, Robert Ellsberg, for his excellent account of this encounter, found in his book All Saints.

BLESSED JUAN DIEGO
Witness to Our Lady of Guadalupe
(sixteenth century)

> "My dear Lady, . . . this I beg you, entrust your mission to one of the important persons who is well known, respected, and esteemed so that they may believe him. You know that I am nobody, a nothing, a coward, a pile of old sticks . . . You have sent me to walk in places where I do not belong. Forgive me and please do not be angry with me, my Lady and Mistress."

On the morning of December 9, 1531, a Christian Indian named Juan Diego was on his way to Mass. As he passed a hill at Tepeyac, not far from present-day Mexico City, he heard a voice calling him by name. Looking up he was surprised to see a young Indian maiden. She instructed him to go to the bishop and tell him to construct a church on this hill, the site of an ancient Nahuatl shrine to the mother goddess. Juan faithfully carried out the assignment, but the bishop paid him no attention. In a subsequent showing the maiden charged him to try again, this time identifying herself as the Mother of God. Again the bishop scoffed. At a third audience with the Lady, she instructed Juan Diego to gather a bouquet of roses which were growing, unseasonably, at her feet. Juan gathered the roses in his tilma, or cape. Having gained another audience with the bishop, who had demanded some kind of sign, Juan Diego opened his tilma to present the flowers. To his astonishment, he discovered a full-color image of the Lady mysteriously imprinted on the rough fabric.

So was born the cult of Our Lady of Guadalupe (as the Indian name of the Lady was rendered in Spanish). But in a deeper sense this apparition marked the birth of the Mexican people—a fusion between the Spanish and the indigenous races and cultures. The apparition to Juan Diego occurred only ten years after the conquest of Mexico, a time when the native Indians were languishing under the impact of their cultural decimation. The conquerors had brought with them the new Christian religion, but under such circumstances that it posed little attraction.

All this changed after Guadalupe. The image of the Lady had dark skin and Indian features. The style and colors of her clothing, her blue mantle covered with stars, her depiction as standing on a crescent moon held aloft by an angel, all these features had deep symbolic references to the Indian religion and culture. She spoke to Juan Diego in his own Nahuatl language—not in Spanish—and presented herself not in terms of power and domination but in terms of compassion and solidarity with the poor. She called herself the "Mother of the true God through whom one lives" and stated her wish to see a temple built at that site so that she could "show and give forth all my love, compassion, help, and defense to all the inhabitants of this land . . . to hear their lamentations and remedy their miseries, pain, and sufferings."

If all this was significant to the Indians, there was also a message to the Spanish. Previously the Spanish had seen no conflict between the mission of conquest and the mission of evangelization. But here a divine message was delivered to the bishop—the official representative of the Spanish church—by means of a humble Indian. In effect, Juan Diego was chosen to be the agent of the bishop's—and the church's—conversion. The message was clear: the church must not serve as the religious arm of colonial oppression. Instead it must be rooted in the experience of the poor and become a vehicle for their cultural and spiritual survival.

Within six years of the apparition nine million Aztecs were baptized. The official church went on to build a rich basilica at Tepeyac and to sponsor the official cult of Our Lady of Guadalupe. Still, in succeeding centuries the image of Guadalupe remained a source of special pride and devotion among the poor, a symbol of God's special love for the oppressed, and of the compassionate face of God revealed in his Mother.

Apart from the official cult, the image of Guadalupe would resurface regularly in more militant and "unauthorized" contexts. Banners with her image were carried by the peasant army of Emiliano Zapata during the Mexican Revolution. Cesar Chavez, leader of the United Farmworkers Union in the United States, carried her image on the picket line. In 1993 Indian peasants supporting the Zapatista uprising in Chiapas, Mexico, marched beneath her banner. The image of Guadalupe continues to hold a special meaning for the humble and oppressed peoples of the Americas. For others she is a potent symbol of the church of the future—a church that celebrates diversity, empowers the poor, and speaks with the voice of compassion. Where such a church lives, roses bloom in December.

ADDENDUM TWO TO MEXICO—A REVERIE

Pope Paul VI wrote "Devotion to the Blessed Virgin is firmly rooted in the revealed word and has solid dogmatic foundations. It is based on the singular dignity of Mary, Mother of the Son of God, and therefore beloved daughter of the Father and Temple of the Holy Spirit—Mary who, because of this extraordinary grace, is far greater than any other creature on earth or in heaven."

PRAYER TO OUR LADY OF GUADALUPE

Our Lady of Guadalupe, Mystical Rose, intercede for the Church, protect the Holy Father, help all who invoke You in their necessities. Since you are the ever Virgin Mary and Mother of the true God, obtain for us from your most Holy Son the grace of a firm and a sure hope amid the bitterness of life, as well as an ardent love and the precious gift of final perseverance.

GREECE—A REVERIE

Ancient Greece is a period in Greek history that lasted for around 3000 years. It is generally considered to be the seminal culture which provided the foundation of Western civilization. Greek culture had a powerful influence on the Roman Empire, which carried a version of it to many parts of Europe. The civilization of the ancient Greeks has been immensely influential on the language, politics, educational systems, philosophy, science, and arts, giving rise to the Renaissance in Western Europe and again resurgent during various neo-Classical revivals in 18th and 19th century Europe and the Americas. Traditionally, the Ancient Greek period was taken to begin with the date of the first recorded Olympic Games in 776 BC. The traditional date for the end of the Ancient Greek period is the death of Alexander the Great in 323 BC. The following period is classed Hellenistic or until the integration of Greece into the Roman Republic in 146 BC. The origins of the Greeks can be found in reference books in any Chicago public library.

For the sake of continuity, let us cite a few events that somewhere along the line we studied or heard about. In 490 BC; during the Persian Wars, the Persian Great King, Darius I, sent a fleet to punish the Greeks. The Persians landed in Attica, but were defeated at the Battle of Marathon by a Greek army led by the Athenian general Miltiades. The burial mound of the Athenian dead can still be seen at Marathon. A Greek soldier ran all the way from Marathon to Athens, a distance of 26 miles, 385 yards to announce the victory to the city-state and completely exhausted immediately dropped dead after announcing the victory!! Ten years later Darius' successor, Xerxes Ist, sent a much more powerful force by land. After being delayed by the Spartan King Leonidas at the mountain pass at Thermopylae which allowed the Athenians to evacuate the city by sea. King Leonidas with 300 soldiers delayed thousands of Persian soldiers. The Spartans all lost their lives saving all of Greece, but it shows what a small dedicated force can do against a much larger and more powerful enemy! After the delay Xerxes advanced into Attica where he captured and burned Athens. But the Athenians had evacuated the city by the sea, and under Themistocles,

61

they defeated the Persian fleet in the Battle of Salamis. A year later, the Greeks, under the Spartan Pausanius, defeated the Persian army at Plataea. The Athenian fleet then turned to chasing the Persians out of the Aegian Sea, and in 478 BC they captured Byzantium. This allowed the city-state of Athens to establish unchallenged naval and commercial power. As you probably know Persia is now the nation of Iran.

The Persian Wars ushered in a century of Athenian dominance of Greek affairs. Athens was the unchallenged master of the sea, as well as the leading commercial power in that part of the world. But now, let us go back in time and introduce Abraham. Abraham was called by God around 1900 BC to found a new nation called the Hebrews (later called the Israelites and finally the Jews). Genesis tells their story and how they ended up as slaves in Egypt. Around 1250 BC, Moses led them out of Egypt and finally they reached the promised land inhabited by the Canaanites. Jews then conquered the many tribes living there and they themselves settled in the land. Turn now to the Old Testament with special attention to the books of Psalms, Proverbs and all the Prophets. The last prophet died sometime in the fifth century BC. Back now to Athens. Since the Athenians were masters of the sea and commerce, they would have undoubtedly known about the Israelites and been familiar with their beliefs and writings. In this way God was using His chosen people to influence the Greeks as they became leaders in politics, philosophy and the arts. In a sense, Greece was also chosen by God to plant the seeds of Christianity which would come to fulfillment with the birth, life, passion, death and resurrection of Jesus Christ. Yes, it is true: What is concealed in the Old Testament is revealed in the New Testament.

Here are just a few quotes of famous Ancient Greeks which clearly show the influence of the Jewish writings:

> *AESOP* (storyteller, used animals to teach moral lessons)
> * No act of kindness, no matter how small, is ever wasted. We should look at a person's mind, not his appearance.
> * There's a time for work and a time for play.
>
> *ARISTOPHANES* (comic playwriter)
> * We're keen to let the judges know just what they'll get if we come in first!
> * You have all the traits of a popular politician: A horrible voice, bad upbringing, and a vulgar manner.
>
> *EPICURUS* (Philosopher)
> * One is never too young or too old to seek wisdom.
>
> *EURIPIDES* (playwrite of 92 plays—he addressed the position of women in Greek society in his most famous works which are Media, Trojan Women and Electra)

Religious Reveries for Retired Residents | 63

- * Only a quiet conscience is able to endure the joys and sorrows of a person's life.
- * Whoever neglects learning when he is young, loses the past and is dead for the future.
- * In a conflict, never judge until you hear both sides.

HOMER (best remembered for the epic poems, The Illiad and The Odyssey)
- * Bards are honored and revered throughout the world, because the Muse has taught them songs and loves the race of bards.
- * Tell me, O Muse, of that man, so in need of help, who wandered far and wide, after he had sacked the sacred city of Troy.

PERICLES OF ATHENS (Statesman—the first to pay government workers and established many democratic reforms)
- * Time is the wisest of all counselors.
- * Outstanding individuals have the whole world as their memorial.
- * Future ages will wonder at us, as the present age wonders at us now.

SOPHOCLES (playwrite and politician—plays Ajax, Antigone, and Oedipus The King still survive)
- * We know the world is a wonderful place and the first of all is the human race.
- * Wisdom outweighs any wealth.
- * When fighting for something that is right, even weakness triumphs.

THALES OF MILETUS (founded the study of philosophy and mathematics and developed the first principles of geometry.)
- * Time is the wisest of things because it finds out everything.

XENOPHON (historian, a student of Socrates)
- * The most pleasing sound is the one that praises you.

And now four of the most famous and talented Greeks of this era:

1. Socrates left no writings or recordings of his beliefs, yet his philosophies still impact Western thought. His students include Plato, Aristophanes, Xenophon, and Aristotle. Plato's dialogues, with a main character, give us a good, if biased account of Socrates' philosophies. He debated morality and how individuals should conduct their lives.

   * Knowledge is the only good and ignorance the only evil.

2. Plato followed the teachings of Socrates and taught Aristotle. He wrote dialogues in which two or more characters discussed their ideas about human nature and government. He used questions to guide one deeper into more serious and abstract thought. His school in Athens was called the Academy.

   *The direction in which education starts an individual determines his future life.

3. Aristotle (384-322 BC) is known as the father of logic. A philosopher, he was a student of Plato's and a tutor to Alexander the Great, established the Lyceum, a college level school in Athens. He wrote hundreds of works on a wide variety of subjects. Some of these were biology, history, physics, literature, ethics, logic, political theory, and rhetoric. He believed that what we perceive with our senses is the "Real Thing."

   * Education is the best provision for old age.
   * Art completes what nature leaves unfinished.
   * By an uneducated man, we mean someone who completely lacks chorus training; the educated man is fully chorus trained.

4. Alexander the Great (356-323 BC) began his conquest of that part of the world in 334 BC when he crossed into Asia and defeated the Persians at the river Granicus. This gave him control of the Ionian coast. He then conquered Anatolia, Syria, Phoenicia, Egypt, Mesopotamia, and pressed on through what is now Afghanistan and Pakistan. He had conquered the world. Alexander died of a fever in Babylon in 323 BC. His empire broke up soon after his death, but his conquests permanently changed the Greek world. Thousands of Greeks traveled with him or after him to settle in the new Greek cities he had founded as he advanced, the most important being Alexandria in Egypt. Greek-speaking kingdoms in Egypt, Syria, Persia and Bactria were established. The knowledge and cultures of east and west began to permeate and interact. The Hellenistic Age (336-146 BC) had begun! But here is a sampling of OT passages that Greeks would have heard or read that had to influence their thinking and discussions:

   * (Deuteronomy 4:1-9) "Therefore, I (Moses) teach you the statutes and decrees as the Lord, my God, has commanded me, that you may observe them in the land you are to occupy. Observe them carefully, for thus will you give evidence of your wisdom and intelligence to the nations, who will hear of all these statutes

and say, "This great nation is truly a wise and intelligent people. For what great nation is there that has gods so close to it as the Lord, our God, is to us whenever we call upon Him? Or what great nation has statutes and decrees that are as just as this whole law which I am setting before you today? Let them never slip from your memory as long as you live, but teach them to your children and to your children's children."

* (Psalm 86) "Lord, there is no god to compare with you; you are great and do wonderful things, you are the only God."
* (Psalm 119:133) Lord, direct my steps as you have promised, and let no evil hold me in its power."

This little example of how the Jewish writings could have influenced the thinking of the Greek intelligentsia and this is why Paul could not help but be impressed with Athens. This was a special city filled with ancient temples and majestic buildings. In many ways, Athens was the home of Western philosophy and what we now know as democracy. The center of the city was the agora, or market place, where the men of Athens met each day to hold discussions about all sorts of topics. Athenians loved to debate and discuss. Even in government assemblies, citizens had a right to speak in their own names, not just through representatives. Paul began telling these people who worshipped many gods about the one and only living God who created the world. Day after day Paul walked around in the market place, unafraid to argue even with the learned Greeks he met there. Paul's unusual ideas created so much interest that he was invited to speak in the council hall called the Areopagus: "The one amusement the Athenians and the foreigners living there seem to have, apart from discussing the latest ideas, is listening to lectures about them (Acts 17:21). Now enjoy re-reading Acts 17:16-34 with perhaps a little more background of the days Paul traveled and preached.

The Greek empire was gradually taken over by the Romans and was absorbed into the Roman empire. To write more on this is beyond the scope of this article. However, it should be emphasized again the great influence the Greeks had on the Christian Church. The Greek philosophers Plato, Socrates, and Aristotal had an enormous impact on Catholic theology. In addition, the Greek Church Fathers, such as St. Athanasius, St. Gregory Nanzianzen, St. Gregory of Nyssa, St. Basil, St. John Chrysostom, and St. John Damascene preserved the true faith from heresy and also greatly influenced the way that the church does theology. Using philosophical terms and logical reasoning they established the revealed faith in a rational and coherent manner. This was considered the great gift of the Greeks in addition to their art and music, icons, and sense of mystery. The Catholic church gave the title "Church Father" to men who lived holy lives before A.D. 800, provided that their doctrines were orthodox, conforming to the official Magisterium.

In A.D. 286 the old Roman Empire was divided into East (Byzantium) and West (Roman). The Emperor Constantine then established the imperial town on Constantinople with its Patriarch as head of the Eastern part of the Roman Empire. When the pope in Rome crowned Charlemagne, King of the Franks, as the Holy Roman Emperor, the Byzantine East saw it as a slap to the Eastern Emperor and the Empire itself. From then on, relations between the East and the West deteriorated until a formal split occurred in 1054 when the schism took place. The Eastern Church became the Greek Orthodox church by severing all ties with Rome and the Roman Catholic church, from the pope to the Holy Roman Emperor on down. Over the centuries, the Eastern Church and the Western Church became more distant and isolated for many reasons, however only those relevant to this paper are mentioned here:

* The West encompassed Western Europe and the northern and western areas of the Mediterranean and the East took of Asia Minor, the Middle East, and Northern Africa.
* The Byzantine Church knew less and less Latin and even less Latin tradition, and vice versa. So most patriarchs in Cosntantinople couldn't read any Latin,a nd most popes in Rome couldn't read any Greek.
* Both had valid theologies but each its own perspective. The West (Latin) was more practical and, although fully believing in the divinity of Christ, put emphasis on His humanity when depicting Jesus in art. The East (Byzantine) was more theoretical and, although fully believing in the humanity of Christ, focused on His divinity, which was more mysterious.
* Michael Cerularius, Patriarch of Constantinople and Pope St. Leo IX weren't friends and each one mistrusted the other.

In the end, Pope Leo and Patriarch Michael excommunicated each other and their respective churches. But more than 900 years later, in 1965, Pope Paul VI and Patriarch Athenagoras I of Constantinople removed the mutual excommunications! John Paul II made many visits to the Greek Orthodox Patriarch and priests to ask for forgiveness and to plead that we all truly become one, in full communion with each other.

Now, gentle reader, let us end our reverie by looking at the Catholic church today in Greece. Population of Greece is about 11,000,000 inhabitants. About 95% of the population belong to the official church of the state which according to Article 3 of Greek constitution is "the Oriental Orthodox church". There is a Muslim minority of about 150,000 in Thraki (towards the frontier with Turkey) a small Jewish Community and various Protestant denominations. Numerous sects of American origin are spreading rapidly. Catholic Greeks number between 45,000 and 50,000 (0.5% of the population) and are a religious minority and not an ethnic minority. Catholics and Orthodox share common forenames and family names, as well as traditions especially on the islands. The contribution of Roman Catholics to neohellenic literature during the last centuries is not negligible. There are difficulties resulting from the fact that Catholics not residing in Athens are dispersed all over the country (mixed marriages, assembling children for catechism, scattered groups of teenagers and young people and other difficulties for the ecclesiastical community). This diaspora, even in large towns, makes the pastoral work of priests and religious very hard. The problem has heightened during the last two decades on account of the decreasing number of priests and religious. The Catholic Church in Greece is viewed by the State as a foreign denomination and must cope with judiciary problems resulting from the existing legal deficiency on this point. In spite of the repeated efforts of the Catholic Hierarchy of Greece addressed to the government during the last 50 years, and the last decade in particular, the state does not seem willing to find a solution to the problems concerning the Catholic Church in Greece. We must underline that the countries of the European Union, as well as other countries in Western and Central Europe, consider the Greek Orthodox Church not only as an equal but even provide salaries to the Orthodox clergy whose members may have foreign passports. However, in Greece we are registered and referred to as Catholic Greek citizens. The request of the Catholic Church in Greece is not for privileges or other special favours, but simply equal Civil Rights for Catholic Greek Citizens, particularly civil servants, as is the case for Greeks living within the European Union, who are predominantly Greek Orthodox.

> Mary, Seat of Wisdom, pray for us
> Mary, Seat of Wisdom, help us to become one.
> Kyrie, Eleison. Christe, Eleison. Kyrie, Eleison.

Bert Hoffman

ADDENDUM ONE TO GREECE—A REVERIE

I made a nine-day private retreat with the Franciscan Friars of the Atonement located on Mount Graymoor. This mountain is completely surrounded by the city of Garrison, New York. You will learn more of Father Paul Wattson, its founder, as you continue reading this addendum. Paul Wattson was a Protestant minister, converted to Roman Catholicism and became a Catholic priest. He was aware of the divisions among the Orthodoxy, Protestantism and Catholicism. He studied the many attempts that had been made for reunion and how they were unsuccessful due to misunderstandings over beliefs intertwined with cultural and ethnic rivalries. Father Paul pondered the words of Jesus "that they may be one, Father, as You and I are one (John 17:21)" and the centuries of living and worshipping apart from each other which encrusted the ugly wounds of Christ's one Church. So to combat this he founded the Franciscan Friars of the Atonement at Graymoor and this is the reason I made my 9 day private retreat. During these 9 days there were 3 other 3-day retreats which I joined and participated in all the sessions, one Orthodox and 2 Protestant. All of us benefited from the sessions and all of us increased our understanding and respect for each others beliefs. We all wished we could become one, the sooner the better. As you read on remember that in all our biblical and prayer sessions some Orthodox, Protestant and Catholic Christians were present and actively participating (please excuse the possible overlapping of some ideas and descriptions). Graymoor is the home of the Franciscan Friars and Sisters of the Atonement. With an array of beautiful chapels and shrines, the mountains and surrounding valley encourage moments of peace and quiet reflection.

In 1898, Father Paul Wattson (always referred to as Father Paul) and Mother Lurana White founded the Society of the Atonement in the Franciscan tradition for the purpose of making humanity at one with itself and at one with God. Today the friars and sisters carry out their mission of at-one-ment in ministries across the U.S., Canada, England, Italy and Japan, but home is here at Graymoor.

Ah, patient reader, forgive this slight digression to St. Francis of Assisi, Founder of the Friars Minor (1182-1226). His life is well worth reading, his feast day in October 4. St. Francis was born in the Umbrian city of Assisi. His parents were Pietro Di Bernardone, a wealthy cloth merchant (could Bishop Bernardine be somehow related? I'll let you research that), and Pica, his French-born wife. Francis was one of the privileged young men of Assisi, attracted to adventure and frivolity as well as tales of romance. I stop here but to satisfy your interest and curiosity you can read any one of his many excellent biographies. But I digressed not to tell you of his life but to tell you about two incidents in his life that relate to Graymoor. (l.) Ultimately Francis attempted no more than to live out the teachings of Christ and the spirit of the Gospel. His identification with Christ was so intense that in 1224, while praying at the altar in his hermitage, he received the "stigmata," the physical marks of Christ's Passion, on his hands and feet! (2.) His last years were marked at once by excruciating physical suffering and spiritual happiness. "Welcome Sister Death!" he exclaimed at last. At his request he was laid on the bare ground in his old habit. To the friars gathered around him he gave each his blessing in turn: "I have done my part," he said. "May Christ teach you to do yours." So he died on October 3, 1226. I repeat his feast again is observed on October 4. His friars made a death mask of St. Francis. Now back to Graymoor. These were my two favorite shrines at Graymoor both were on top of mount Graymoor where I spent most of my solitary time in prayers and reflections: (1.) The tomb of Father Paul, dedicated in October 1971, and occupying a spot Father Paul called Calvary Rock, his tomb bears the words of Christ, "that they all may be one," which compelled him to spend his entire life praying and working for Christian Unity. A replica of Michalangelo's Pieta looks over the tomb. Beyond the Pieta is a spectacular view of the Hudson Valley and the distant New York City skyline. (2.) St. Francis Chapel, about 30 feet away form the tomb is hailed as Garymoors most beautiful Chapel. This Chapel was built by the homeless men of St. Christopher's Inn with a bell tower resembling that of St. Francis Basilica in Assisi. Appraised as a "museum piece," this altar once marked the spot on Mount Alverna in Assisi where St. Francis received the stigmata in 1224. The Diocese of Assisi sent this altar to Graymoor in the early 1900s. The statue of St. Anthony which is at its side is where the Perpetual Novena to St. Anthony began in 1912. Among the stained glass windows are two of Our Lady of the Atonement and a large one of St. Cecilia. There have only been two statues sculptured of St. Francis using the death mask made by the Friars at the time of his death, one is in San Damiano, Assisi, and the other the Diocese of Assisi sent to Graymoor, again in the early 1900's, and now proudly stands above the altar, very easy to see, it is the pride of Graymoor! Tucked under the Chapel's extended roof sits the "Palace of Lady Poverty," a paint shack, where Father Paul first lived after his arrival at Graymoor in 1899. He named it in honor of St. Francis who referred to evangelical poverty as Lady Poverty. On July 27, 1900, Father Paul made his vows of poverty, chastity, and obedience near this chapel. Also near by was the site of Mother Lurana's profession of vows, the First Church Unity Octave observance in 1908 (now known as the Week of Prayer for Christian unity) and the reception of the Society of the Atonement into the Roman Catholic Church in 1909.

Before going on, let me say that if I can make a retreat, so can you, and by the way, these are NOT silent retreats! However, there are scheduled times set aside for private meditations. I usually found myself thinking of my past life, thinking of all the people I met in my life and the things we did and the fun we had together, thinking of what God wants me to do as I continue on my pilgrimage through life. You really do get to know yourself a little better. Well, if you have never made a retreat you might like to try it. Simply write to

>Father James Gardiner, SA
>Graymoor
>P.O. Box 300
>Route 9
>Garrison, New York 10524-0300
>Telephone # 1-800-338-2620

Now, let's complete ADDENDUM ONE.

1. This article was written by George Weigel for the April 15-28, 2007 issue of the Catholic New World (Chicago Archdiocese). George Weigel is a senior fellow of the Ethics and Public Policy Center in Washington, D.C.

Reconciliation with Orthodox Church is not simple.

Last December's visit by Pope Benedict XVI to Ecumenical Patriarch Bartholomew of Constantinople revived speculation that the millennium-long division between Rome and the Christian East might soon end. That was certainly the dream of Benedict's predecessor, the Servant of God John Paul II, who really did seem to believe that Rome and Constantinople could achieve ecclesial reconciliation by the end of the twentieth century, so that a millennium of division—the formal split having taken place in 1054—would be succeeded by a new millennium of unity, in a return to the relations that prevailed in the first centuries of Christian history. It was a noble vision, but it may not have accurately measured the depth of the chasm between Catholicism and some parts of the worlds-within-worlds of Orthodoxy. Recent comments on Benedict's December pilgrimage by the Orthodox monks of Mount Athos suggest that the division is deep and wide indeed.

Mount Athose, a craggy peninsula in northern Greece, is home to 20 self-governing Orthodox monasteries. In fact, Mount Athos is virtually a country unto itself; its formal designation in Greece is the "Autonomous Monastic State of the Holy mountain." No women or female animals are allowed on Mount Athos; visitors are strictly limited; only male members of the Orthodox Church may become monks. And, while Mount Athos comes under the ecclesiastical jurisdiction of the Ecumenical Patriarchate of Constantinople, the Athonite monks, who regard their monasticism as what they term "the non-negotiable guardian of the Holy Tradition," were very unhappy with Ecumenical Patriarch Bartholomew and the way he treated his Roman guest in December.

Why? Because, the monks complained, "the Pope was received as though he were the canonical bishop of Rome." There were other complaints, but that was the first listed in a statement released last December 30 by the Assembly of Representatives and Superiors of the 20 monasteries: Why was Bartholomew treating Benedict as though the latter were, in fact, the bishop of Rome?

Well, if we can't agree on that, we do have, as Jim Lovell told Mission Control, a problem.

To be sure, Athonite monasticism, "the non-negotiable guardian of the Holy Tradition," is a particularly stringent form of Orthodoxy. And if the monks of Mount Athos have their dubieties about the ecumenical openness of Patriarch

Bartholomew, it is, perhaps, not surprising that they imagine Benedict XVI as a usurper and a teacher of heresies. Yet this Athonite intransigence reflects a hard truth about Catholic-Orthodox relations after a millennium of division: namely, that, for many Orthodox Christians, the statement "I am not in communion with the Bishop of Rome" has become an integral part of the statement, "I am an Orthodox Christian."

The obverse is not true. I very much doubt that there are more than a handful of Catholics around the world whose confession of Catholic faith includes, as a key component, "I am not in communion with the Patriarch of Constantinople."

The truth of the matter is that, outside historically Orthodox countries and certain ethnic communities, the thought of how one stands vis-à-vis the Patriarch of Constantinople simple doesn't enter Catholic heads. Perhaps that's a problem, but it's nowhere near as great an obstacle to ecumenical progress as the conviction in some Orthodox quarters that non-communion with Rome is a defining characteristic of what it means to be "Orthodox."

1054, it now seems clear, was not a date-in-a-vacuum. Rather, the mutual excommunications of 1054 were the cash out, so to speak, of a drifting-apart that had been going on for centuries, driven by language and politics, to be sure, but also by different theological sensibilities. Are those two sensibilities necessarily church dividing? The Catholic answer is, "No." But that is emphatically not the answer of Mount Athos, and of those Orthodox for whom the Athonite monks are essentially right, if a bit over-the-top.

All of which suggests that John Paul II's dream of a church breathing once again with both of its lungs is unlikely of fulfillment anytime soon. Unless, that is, Islamist pressures compel a reexamination within orthodoxy of what a life-line to Rome might mean.

2. This article was written by Bishop Demetrios of Mokissos, Chancellor, Greek Orthodox metropolis of Chicago, for the May 15, 2007 issue of The Catholic New World (Chicago Archdiocese).

Christ is Risen!

In regard to the article by George Weigel, "Reconciliation with Orthodox church is not simple," I would like to make the following observations from an Orthodox perspective.

I do appreciate that the author considers reconciliation between the two sister churches, separated by many centuries of schism, to be an important subject. Unfortunately, in an attitude that may be widespread, he betrays a one-sided notion of what reconciliation means when he predicates this on a "reexamination within Orthodoxy of what a life-line to Rome might mean." He suggests that "Islamist pressures" may precede this.

"Islamist pressures" have not been and should not be the motivation for reconciliation between "sister" churches in schism. Indeed, when such pressures were present in the Byzantine era, moves to reunite Easy and West failed since their foundation was not love and concord in the Faith. For several centuries, Orthodoxy survived in Europe under the Ottoman yoke, and still survives as the faith of a minority in several nations of the Middle East where Islam is the faith of the majority. At times, there have been and continue to be persecutions overt or subtle, yet the Orthodox Church has witnessed to the truth and thereby survived. The only true motivation for reunion between the Church of Rome and the Orthodox Churches must be mutual faith, concord and love, "that they may be one" (Jn 17:11). Any other motivation—economic, political or otherwise—would only amount to a false union founded on the "cares of this life" (Luke 21:34) and not concern for the communion of the everlasting Kingdom.

Likewise, Orthodoxy does not require a "life-line to Rome" as the author suggests. While the author laments a lack of recognition of the canonicity of the Bishop of Rome by the monastics of Mount Athos, his own view of Orthodoxy is not substantially different. If Orthodoxy requires Rome for life and vitality, she must not be the living Body of Christ. This, of course, is an ecclesiological position that precludes viewing Rome and the Orthodox as true "sister churches." And this precludes reconciliation.

Undoubtedly, Mr. Weigel is correct to lament the continued distrust and suspicion of Rome present in some parts of the orthodox Church. However, he is incorrect to think that schism with Rome is integral to the self-identity of Athonite monasticism in particular or Orthodox Christians in general. The history of mutual distrust, suspicion, violence, recrimination and even persecution is too complex to dismiss.

In Eastern Europe (including the Ukraine as well as Greece), cultural memory lingers far longer than in the West (especially our own nation), and the pain of schism—while not defining of one's own tradition—cannot go unnoticed. Mr. Weigel admits this pain is felt even among Roman Catholics in the region. But the protest of the Athonite monks reflects not only a caution arising from such pain, but primarily the "different theological sensibilities" to which Mr. Weigel refers. One of these is our sense of communion that transcends national boundaries and "certain ethnic communities." The plight of our fellow Orthodox is shared by us all, regardless of geographic location.

Simply put, Mr. Weigel does not understand Orthodox sensibilities or attitudes, cultural or theological. This is a reason that schism grew in the first place. While Orthodox may be more conscious of the lack of communion with Rome, this may not be so negative as Mr. Weigel implies. This means, at least, perception of the problem. Perhaps the thought of "how one stands vis-à-vis the Patriarch of Constantinople" and other Orthodox primates should be on the minds of more Roman Catholic sisters and brothers. Perhaps then the absence of "one lung" will be recognized as a debilitative condition, while the necessity of communion and reconciliation with Rome's sisters will be felt to be a serious need. Without the perception of brokenness, there can be no change of mind. Without the perception of need for change, without the desire to fill the absence, reconciliation will not occur.

ADDENDUM TWO TO GREECE—A REVERIE

In Russian Orthodox Church
By Paul Likoudis (June, 2007)

In a three-hour ceremony in Moscow's Christ the Savior Cathedral, miraculously rebuilt from 1990-2000 after Stalin demolished it in 1931, the patriarch of the Russian Orthodox Church and representatives of the Russian Orthodox Church Outside Russia (ROCOR), formed in the 1920s at the height of the Bolshevik persecution and the enslavement of the official Church, agreed to end the formal schism that has divided them since.

The restoration of the Russian Orthodox Church's unity has been a preoccupation of Russian President Vladimir Putin, who was secretly baptized by his mother after his birth in Stalin's reign.

After the ceremony, which was televised across the country—officially marking the end of the Bolshevik era, according to some observers—President Putin said the "restoration of Church unity has not only an internal Church significance, but it is also an important spiritual stimulus for consolidating the entire 'Russian world'."

"It is this unity that has enabled the Church in all times to take a most active part in building and fostering the millennium-old Russian statehood, to be a pillar and source of its moral and spiritual traditions," he added.

Under the terms of the agreement signed May 17 by patriarch Alexy and Metropolitan Laurus of New York, the Act of Canonical Communion, the Church Ouside of Russia will retain its independence in organizational and financial matters, while it concedes the appointment of metropolitans to the patriarch in Moscow.

Putin described the signing of the accord as "an important spiritual stimulus for consolidating the entire Orthodox, the entire Russian world—the world which was tragically divided as a result of the tragic events and the civil war."

Putin lamented that the civil war forced millions of Russians "not by their own will . . . to leave their Motherland," and he noted the severe trials they endured "in emigration to be able to give a proper appreciation to the mission of the Russian Orthodox Church abroad."

"This church has not simply preserved the purity of the robes, as they say, but also fulfilled her duty before God and the Russian people," he added.

"The restoration of canonical communion is only a first step in mutual rapprochement. There are many consequences of the division to be overcome yet and to restore the lost ties of our compatriots with their Motherland.

"And on the whole,k there is work ahead to foster the unity of the people both inside and outside Russia."

The Holy See hailed the unity agreement. Walter Cardinal Casper, president of the Pontifical Council for the Promotion of Christian Unity, conveyed a letter from pope Benedict XVI to Alexy II.

"We are by no means indifferent to the suffering of your church, tragically divided over the Communist ideology and its grim consequences, and we understand and share the great joy Russian Orthodox communities and others feel today," the letter said.

"We are convinced that such initiatives are right in the advancement toward increasingly complete Christian relations."

The ending of the schism between the two major branches of the Russian Orthodox Church, however, raises interesting doctrinal questions, said James Likoudis, an expert on Catholic-Orthodox relations.

"First," he said, "ROCOR has been violently opposed to ecumenism, such as Orthodox participation in the World Council of Churches, of which the patriarchal Church has been a member. Furthermore, ROCOR is opposed to formal Orthodox-Catholic dialog, on the grounds that Catholics are heretics, and their spokesmen have even denied Catholics have valid sacraments; whereas the patriarchal Church regards them as valid."

"A question, for Catholics, is: 'What does this ending of the schism mean in terms of a resolution of the doctrinal differences that have existed between these two jurisdictions?' Certainly the Catholic Church is not interested in the maintaining of schisms among her separated brethren.

"But," he added, "it will be interesting to observe whether there will occur even more schisms among the Orthodox who have been most opposed to Catholic-Orthodox rapprochement."

The Russian Orthodox Church Outside Russia, which now operates some 400 parishes and 20 major monasteries worldwide, primarily in the United States, Australia, Austria, Germany, the United Kingdom, and South America, was formed in 1927, after the imprisoned Moscow patriarch Sergiy recognized the legitimacy of the Bolshevik government. Exiled hierarchs, most of whom had fled to Siberia or Manchuria, then formed ROCOR, on the basis that the Moscow Patriarch had become a puppet of the Soviet state.

The hierarchs of ROCOR, however, insisted it was the true Great Russian Church, and not a separate branch.

After the breakup of the Soviet Union, ROCOR insisted on maintaining its independence from a reinvigorated Moscow Patriarchate, on the grounds that the Moscow patriarchate was honeycombed with KGB agents.

In 2000, Metropolitan Laurus of New York became ROCOR's first hierarch, and expressed interest in ending the schism, if the Moscow patriarch would apologize for its subservience to the Soviet politburo and address the assassination of Czar Nicholas, whom ROCOR considered a saint, and address the issue of dialogue with the Church of Rome, which it considered heretical.

In 2003 Vladimir Putin met with Metropolitan Laurus in New York, an event regarded by Patriarch Alexy as indicating that Laurus was an "Orthodox Christian."

On May 12, 2006, the general congress of the ROCOR confirmed its willingness to reunite with the Russian Orthodox Church, which hailed this resolution as "an important step toward restoring full unity between the Moscow patriarchate and the part of the Russian emigration that was isolated from it as a result of the revolution, the civil war in Russia, and the ensuing impious persecution against the Orthodox Church."

At the May 17 service at Christ the Savior Cathedral, President Putin praised the reconciliation between the two branches, saying: "The split in the church was caused by an extremely deep political split within Russian society itself. We have realized that national revival and development in Russia are impossible without reliance on the historical and spiritual experience of our people. We understand well, and value, the power of pastoral words which unite the people of Russia. That is why restoring the unity of the Church serves our common goals."

U.S.A.—A REVERIE

The colonists were assured their rights and privileges as Englishmen which traces back to 1215 when King John was compelled by the feudal nobles to sign the Great Charter, or Magna Carta, would be preserved. In time Magna Carta came to mean that (a) the king is not an absolute ruler but is subject to the laws, (b) all persons are guaranteed trial by jury, (c) Parliament alone may levy taxes. The English colonists expected these rights which by the 18th century had been greatly expanded to apply to them in America. After England had defeated France in the French and Indian War, the Treaty of Paris (1763) eliminated France as a colonial power in North America; that is, France was no longer a threat to the colonists, in other words the colonists had no longer a need for the British army and navy. Also starting in 1763, the British government adopted a new colonial policy including (1) placing the colonies under strict British political and economic control, (2) to make the colonies bear a major part of the cost of maintaining the British Empire since England was rather broke following the war with France, and (3) to compel the colonists to demonstrate respect for and obedience to English laws.

Parliament, however, passed many acts and taxes opposed by the colonies; here are a few examples: Navigation Acts but merchants and ship owners continued to smuggle goods into the colonies to avoid import duties; lawyers and writers protested the writs of assistance (search warrants) as illegal invasions of colonial property. Appearing before a Boston court, James Otis (1761) eloquently but unsuccessfully denounced the writs for violating the English common law principle that "a man's home is his castle." Otis argued that there was a higher fundamental (divine) right that a man's privacy could not be invaded and that Divine law was higher than Parliamentary law. Then two years later, in 1763, in the Parson's cause in which the salary of the clergy was changed from being paid in tobacco to being paid in pence by an emergency law passed by the Parliament resulting in a 75% loss in the clergy's salary. Patrick Henry defended the clergy in Virginia—"They were being cheated out of their wage."

Patrick Henry argued in almost the same light as James Otis—"Neither the king nor the privy council can regulate the internal governments; there is a law higher than the king to allow colonists to rule themselves. These people believed that they had those natural rights. Both Otis and Henry lost their cases, but what was significant was that in two removed cases, both lawyers thought the same way without knowing each other. This was the prevalent attitude in the colonies. That was what John Adams meant when he later said in the First Continental Congress (Philadelphia, 1774) "The revolution was over, it just took a war to prove it." In Virginia, that same Patrick Henry acclaimed the work of the Continental Congress in a famous speech, concluding with: "I know not what course others may take but as for me, give me liberty or give me death." Realizing that liberty might require defense, colonial patriots began training militiamen and storing military supplies.

In Massachusetts the British general Thomas Gage ordered a detachment of troops to seize colonial military supplies at Concord and to arrest the colonial leaders John Hancock and Samuel Adams, believed to be at Lexington. Forewarned by Paul Revere ("Listen my children and you shall hear of the midnight ride of Paul Revere . . . one if by land, two if by sea"). Minutemen, who were Massachusetts militiamen pledged to be ready at a minutes notice, were waiting to resist the British troops. Fighting broke out. As the poet Ralph Waldo Emerson later said, "Here once the embattled farmers stood and fired the shot heard round the world." Thus started the American Revolution! We can look in any history book to read about these war years; its battles and heroics of the colonists before and during the Revolutionary War, but to better understand these days, remember that approximately one-third of the colonists wanted independence, one-third wanted to stay with England (Loyalists), and one-third didn't care one way or the other. What follows, gentle reader, is a brief survey of the Revolutionary War:

1. British successes in the middle States (1776-1777). Britain, a major military power, expected to subdue her rebellious subjects with little difficulty. Under Sir William Howe, a sizable British army sailed into New York Harbor, defeated George Washington's poorly trained forces, and occupied New York City. Washington retreated into New Jersey, where he regained morale-boosting triumphs at Trenton and Princeton. Thereafter, the British redcoats defeated the colonial forces in several engagements near Philadelphia and occupied that city.
2. American victory at Saratoga (1777). In upstate New York, at Saratoga, the Americans defeated and captured General "Gentleman Johnny" Burgoyne and his entire army, which had come southward from Canada. The battle of Saratoga was the turning point of the war. It convinced the French government that the Americans had a chance of winning

the war. Until then, France had been providing the colonists with loans and munitions secretly. Now the French government, heeding our minister, Benjamin Franklin, recognized American independence and in 1778 signed a treaty of alliance with the new nation.

3. American suffering at Valley Forge (1777-1778). Meanwhile, having lost Philadelphia to the British, Washington and his men retreated some 20 miles away to Valley Forge. Inadequately fed and clothed, they suffered through an especially harsh winter. Washington held his army together only with great difficulty. A famous painting shows the father of our country on bended knee in prayer, praying to the Father of all creation during that cold, snowy winter.

4. American victory in the Northwest Territory (1778-1779). George Rogers Clark led a force of less than 200 frontiersmen down the Ohio River and into the western lands. Clark won a series of victories against British garrison forces, climaxed by the recapture of Vincennes. Clark's exploits ended British control of the Northwest Territory and established American claims to the area.

5. War in the South (1778-1781). The British left Philadelphia in 1778 and returned to New York City. Part of the British forces next moved southward. The British won several battles and occupied the major seaport cities of Savannah and Charleston. However, they could not crush the American forces. By early 1781 in the interior of the Carolinas, the British had suffered a series of reversals. British General Charles Cornwallis eventually withdrew northward to Yorktown, Virginia.

6. Yorktown: The final American victory (1781). By 1781 Washington's forces in the New York area had been augmented by a French army under the command of General Rochambeau. Also, a French navy, under Navy Commander DeGrasse, was moving northward from the West Indies. With Cornwallis sitting at Yorktown, Washington quickly moved his forces southward to overwhelm the British on land while the French navy cut off any possible British troops by sea. Cornwallis surrendered, and the war was practically ended. The peace treaty was signed two years later in Paris (1783). The American negotiators were Benjamin Franklin, John Jay, and John Adams and they secured a highly favorable treaty of peace with Britain. Franklin followed his own adage "He who would sell an ounce of freedom for a pound of security deserves neither freedom nor security". Britain recognized the thirteen American states as independent. The new nation was bounded (a) on the north by Canada and the Great Lakes, (b) on the south by Spanish-owned Florida, (c) on the east by the Atlantic Ocean, and (d) on the west by the Mississippi River. The Americans retained their previous rights to fish on the banks off Newfoundland.

But let us begin to end this particular reverie by looking at two army officers in the war that General Washington particularly trusted and respected. The first was Nathan Hale (1755-1776) who was asked by General Washington to spy on the British forces. He was eventually caught and executed as a spy. But this young officer was a hero in the American Army and is honored today as a hero in the courtyard of the Chicago Tribune on North Michigan Avenue with a life size statue on whose base can be read his last words before his execution: "I only regret that I have but one life to lay down for my country."

The other officer was General Benedict Arnold. He was the outstanding General in bringing about the surrender of Burgoyne in the battle of Saratoga, where he was seriously wounded. He slowly recovered and then joined Washington at Valley Forge. Washington at Arnold's request gave him the command of West Point, a position of great strategic importance on the Hudson River. Arnold, deeply involved in debt, and unable to collect from Congress for expenditures he had made during the campaign against Quebec, sadly turned informer. From the early summer of 1779 on, Clinton had been fully apprised of the American plans and movements of troops. Arnold had asked for West Point only because he wished to betray it to the British. Fortunately, the Major Andre conspiracy was discovered in September 1780, Arnold promptly fled to the British and Major Andre was executed. The loss of West Point, which would have cost the Americans control of the whole Hudson Valley, was avoided, but the whole episode was a sad blow to American morale. Clinton found work for Arnold to do in laying waste the Virginia plantations. At the end of the war, Arnold escaped to England where he died very disillusioned, very lonely and ostracized from English society. Perhaps the last lines of Sir Walter Scott's poem, "Breathes there the man with soul so dead, who ne'er to himself has said" Best describes Benedict Arnold's last days:

> High though his titles, proud his name,
> Boundless his wealth as wish can claim,
> Despite those titles, power and pelf,
> The wretch, concentred all in self,
> Living, shall forfeit fair renown,
> And, doubly dying, shall go down
> To the vile dust from whence he sprung,
> Unwept, unhonored, and unsung.

Benedict Arnold is a good example of what happens when EVIL begins to enter into the lives of people. The same is true for nations. Now let us look at our own country and see what happened when evil slowly crept into the lives of our citizens and into our government. Our revolution was fought for true freedom acknowledging that all men are created equal, endowed by their creator with certain inalienable rights, that among these are LIFE, LIBERTY, and THE PURSUIT OF HAPPINESS. Sadly, on January 22, 1973, Evil, real Evil, crept into our nation via the U.S. Supreme Court's Roe v Wade decision that legalized the murder of U.S. Citizens in the womb of their mothers. Since that infamous decision more than 47 million American citizens have been murdered! So, let all RRCers pray that our beloved country returns to the culture of life and to the lofty ideals of our founding fathers found in our Declaration of Independence (1776) and our Constitution (1789). Roe vs Wade will eventually be reversed (a prediction). This reversal (also another prediction) could possibly require each of the fifty States to build a new building or to convert an existing building to serve as a home for unwed mothers. As our Nation slowly becomes the country God wanted us to be, these homes would no longer be needed. Thanks be to God!

Let us end this reverie by looking at the last sentence of the Declaration of Independence: "And, for the support of this declaration, with a firm reliance on the protection of Divine Providence, we mutually pledge to each other our lives, our fortunes, and our sacred honor."

Saint Patrick's High School Theatre Department presented 1776 in its performing Arts Centre, May4-13, 2007. Here is what Kevin Long, theatre program director wrote:

> The musical 1776 is vital for everyone to see. The show is not a history lesson, but a passionate story of the patriotic, very human men who struggled to found this nation. The birth of democracy was not easy. It wasn't neat and clean. These men were naïve visionaries who were able to unite, at the possible cost of their lives, around the principle of liberty they all recognized as greater than themselves. This country's declaration of independence was finally agreed upon because these brave men stopped and said, "We can't allow ourselves to be treated this way any longer. We must stand up for the rights of ourselves and of our descendants." Everyone knows the ending, and yet, the show builds such tension that I sincerely hope you will be on the edge of your seat.

I strongly believe it is time for us to revisit this musical in light of what is currently happening in the world. Current polls suggest that Americans have lost faith in our leaders. The results of our most recent election can attest to this statement. The spirit of these men in 1776 seems remote to us now. However, when we watch the musical, it is an inspiration, a judgment, and a relief to know that America once had such leaders.

A simple courier in the story sings a song called "Mama Look Sharp." This ballad of a dying soldier reminds us that while Congress argued, young men died.

As George Washington states in a dispatch to the Congress, "The eve of battle in New York is near at hand . . . As I write these words, the enemy is plainly in sight beyond the river. How it will end only Providence can direct—but dear God! What brave men I shall lose before this business ends." To this John Adams says, "Time's running out! Get up! Get out of your chair! Tomorrow is here." This show speaks as strongly to us today as it did when it opened in 1969. Enjoy!

Let us celebrate this Fourth of July by lifting our hearts and mind to Almighty God and ask Him to continue to bless and protect our beloved country and that we find the will of God in our lives and in our country!

AMERICA

My country, tis of thee, sweet land of liberty,
Of thee I sing; land where my fathers died,
Land of the pilgrams' pride. From ev'ry
Mountain side let freedom ring!

My native country thee, land of the noble free,
Thy name I love; I love thy rocks and rills,
Thy woods and templed hills; my heart with
Rapture thrills, like that above.

Let music swell the breeze, and ring from all the trees
Sweet freedom's song; let mortal tongues awake;
Let all that breathe partake; let rocks their
Silence break, the sound prolong.

Our Fathers' God, to thee, author of liberty,
To thee we sing; long may our land be bright
With freedom's holy light; protect us
By thy might, Great God, our King.

God Bless America
Bert Hoffman

ADDENDUM TO U.S.A.—A REVERIE

The following reverie was written by me in July, 2006. It shows
how my thoughts were just beginning to develop concerning
the moral and spiritual battle being waged in our country
and how my thoughts had solidified by July, 2007.

FREEDOM—A REVERIE
By: Bert Hoffman

"THE TRUTH WILL SET YOU FREE." We have been truly set free in the spiritual world only by Jesus Christ when He said "I am the Way, the Truth and the Life." His words and actions are this truth. Our founding fathers all believed this. Notice a few representative statements illustrating this fact:

> "Reason and experience both forbid us to expect that national morality can prevail in exclusion of religious principle. Promote, then, as an object of primary importance, institutions for the general diffusion of knowledge." GEORGE WASHINGTON

> "The only foundation for a useful education in a republic is to be laid in religion. Without this there can be no virtue, and without virtue there can be no liberty, and liberty is the object and life of all republican governments. Without religion, I believe that learning does real mischief to the morals and principles of mankind." BENJAMIN RUSH

> "It is religion and morality alone which can establish the principles upon which freedom can securely stand. Religion and virtue are the only foundations of republicanism and of all free governments." JOHN ADAMS

> "Only a virtuous people are capable of freedom. As nations become corrupt and vicious, they have more need of masters." BENJAMIN FRANKLIN

> "The practice of morality being necessary for the well-being of society, He (God) has taken care to impress its precepts so indelibly on our hearts that they shall not be effaced by the subtleties of our brain. We all agree in the obligation of the moral precepts of Jesus and no where will they be found delivered in greater purity than in His discourses." THOMAS JEFFERSON

Shortly after our revolutionary war, Alexis DeTocquerville, a French philosopher, traveled to America to discover what made America great. While inspecting the country, he observed church steeples in every hamlet, village, town and city rising to the heavens." This prompted him to write "America will be great as long as America is good but if America ceases to be good, America will cease to be great." The vast majority of Americans are good, but fellow RCer's. Do you think America as a nation today is good?

What can we do about it? Here is what Abraham Lincoln said in Gettysberg (1863) when he declared that the United States had been conceived in liberty and dedicated to the proposition that all men are created equal," and he urged Americans to "highly resolve that government of the people, by the people, for the people, shall not perish from the earth."

The virtue which had been infused into the Constitution of the United States was no other than the concretion of those abstract principles which had been first proclaimed in the Declaration of Independence and embodied in our Constitution. Abraham Lincoln reminded the nation of this truth with these words: "These communities, by their representatives in Old Independence Hall, said to the whole world of men: "We hold these truths to be self-evident: that all men are created equal; that they are endowed by their Creator with certain inalienable rights; that among these are life, liberty, and the pursuit of happiness."

The U.S. Supreme Court in 1897 openly affirmed this interdependent relationships _____ these two documents when it declared: "The Constitution is but the body and the letter of which the Declaration of Independce is the thought and the spirit, and it is always safe to read the letter of the Constitution in the spirit of the Declaration of Independence."

I invite all of you now to think back to your classrooms where you were first taught that freedom is the ability to become what you should become. To be free is to be able to become what you should, or ought to become. Liberty allows you, makes it possible to do this, to become what you should become, or in other words, liberty allows you to be free.

Our country's motto "In God We Trust" invites us to prayer, so let us all pray, especially as we celebrate the 4th, that our great country will remain the land of the free and the home of the brave.

But now, unfortunately there are forces in our country fighting to control and change our culture from Christianity to Secularism. So let us persevere in the struggle to remain a Christian country by doing everything to aid the spiritual army of God. John Paul II told us "Be not afraid" and asked all of us to return to the recitation of the rosary asking our Blessed Mother Mary, for her intercession. The world has implored her help many times in the past, especially when Christianity and/or the family were under attack by evil forces, and she always answered our prayers!

> O Lord, we bring before you the distress and
> Dangers of peoples and nations. The pleas of
> The imprisoned and the captive; the sorrow of
> The grief stricken, the needs of the refugees and
> the weak, the weariness of the despondent, and
> the weaknesses of the aging. O Lord, stay close
> to all of them. Amen

As we see our flag unfurl in the breeze of freedom this fourth of July, let us again proclaim proudly

> I pledge allegiance to the flag of the United States Of America and to the republic for which it stands, one nation, under God, indivisible, with liberty and justice for all.

ADDENDUM TWO TO U.S.A.—A REVERIE

This article was written by Father John Dietzen (Peoria, Il.) for the July, 2007, issue of The Catholic New World, Archdiocese of Chicago.

Canonization, profiles of North American saints

We read that the first officially recognized Brazilian saint was recently canonized. What exactly does canonization mean? How many Americans have been canonized? Are others to be canonized soon?

> Canonization is a formal declaration by the church that a deceased member of the Christian community is with God in eternal glory and may be venerated in the public worship of the church.

During early Christian centuries only martyrs were so honored. In the fourth century others who lived exemplary holy lives even if they were not killed for their faith ("confessors") began to be venerated as saints too.

Seven canonization processes involving men and women in what is now the United States have been completed, all since 1930.

The first involved eight Jesuit missionaries (six priests, a lay volunteer and a lay brother) known collectively as the North American martyrs. They are Sts. John de Brebeuf, Charles Garnier, Antoine Daniel, Isaac Jogues, Noel Chabanel, Gabriel Lalemant, John Lalande and Rene Goupil. They are commemorated together on October 19.

All were French missionaries who worked and suffered martyrdom between 1642 and 1649 in New France, which included eastern parts of present-day Canada and the United States.

St. Frances Cabrini, founder of the Missionary Sisters of the Sacred Heart, came to America from Italy in 1889 and was canonized in 1946. Her feast is November 13.

St. Elizabeth Ann Seton, a native of New York, was raised Episcopalian, was widowed and left bankrupt with five children at the age of 29. Two years later she joined the Catholic Church. St. Elizabeth is often considered the founder of the Catholic school system in our country. She died in 1821 and was canonized in 1975. January 4 is her feast day.

St. Rose Philippine Duchesne came to the United States as a missionary from France. She established several schools, worked extensively with Native American Indians in later life and was canonized in 1988. Her fest is November 18.

St. John Nepomucene Neumann, Bohemian by birth, was ordained in New York in 1836 as a member of the Redemptorist Congregation. He became the fourth bishop of Philadelphia in 1852. Canonized in 1977, his feast is January 5.

St. Katharine Drexel, born into a wealthy Philadelphia family, spent her life establishing schools for black and American Indian Children. She founded Xavier University in Louisiana, the only historically black Catholic university in our country. She was canonized in 2000 and is commemorated on March 3.

Mother Theodore Guerin, a French nun who ministered in the American "west" (Indiana and Illinois) for 16 years, founded the Sisters of Providence and what is now St. Mary of the Woods University near Terre Haute, Indiana. Canonized in 2006, her feast is celebrated October 3.

Several men and women who are either natives of or worked in North America have been beatified (declared "blessed"). Among them is Kateri Tekakwitha (1656-1680), a Mohawk Indian, the first American Indian and the first American lay person to be beatified.

While their process continues, if or when any of these might be canonized is uncertain.

ADDENDUM THREE TO U.S.A.—A REVERIE

When Father Dietzen mentioned Kateri Tekakwitha, I checked with my friend Father Pat McCloskey, O.F.M., Associate Editor of St. Anthony Messenger and author of "Day by Day with Followers of Francis and Clare (St. Anthony Press). He referred me to his book "Saint of the Day." Here is his biography on Blessed Kateri Tekakwitha, Virgin (1656-1680). Her memorial is July 14 (U.S.A.).

The blood of martyrs is the seed of saints. Nine years after the Jesuits Isaac Jogues and John de Brebeuf were tortured to death by Huron and Iroquois Indians, a baby girl was born near the place of their martyrdom, Auriesville, New York. She was to be the first person born in North America to be canonized. Her mother was a Christian Algonquin, taken captive by the Iroguois and given as wife to the chief of the Mohawk clan, the boldest and fiercest of the Five Nations. When she was four, Kateri lost her parents and little brother in a smallpox epidemic that left her disfigured and half blind. She was adopted by an uncle, who succeeded her father as chief. He hated the coming of the Blackrobes (missionaries), but could do nothing to them because a peace treaty with the French required their presence in villages with Christian captives. She was moved by the words of three Blackrobes who lodged with her uncle, but fear of him kept her from seeking instruction. She refused to marry a Mohawk brave and at 19 finally got the courage to take the step of converting. She was baptized with the name Kateri (Catherine) on Easter Sunday.

Now she would be treated as a slave. Because she would not work on Sunday, she received no food that day. Her life in grace grew rapidly. She told a missionary that she often meditated on the great dignity of being baptized. She was powerfully moved by God's love for human beings and saw the dignity of each of her people. She was always in danger, for her conversion and holy life created great opposition. On the advice of a priest, she stole away one night and began a 200-mile walking journey to a Christian Indian village at Sault St. Louis, near Montreal.

For three years she grew in holiness under the direction of a priest and an older Iroquois woman, giving herself totally to God in long hours of prayer, in charity and in strenuous penance. At 23 she took a vow of virginity, an unprecedented act for an Indian woman, whose future depended on being married. She found a place in the woods where she could pray an hour a day—and was accused of meeting a man there! Her dedication to virginity was instinctive: She did not know about religious life for women until she visited Montreal. Inspired by this, she and two friends wanted to start a community, but the local priest dissuaded her. She humbly accepted an "ordinary" life. She practiced extremely severe fasting as penance for the conversion of her nation. She died the afternoon before Holy Thursday. Witnesses said that her emaciated face changed color and became like that of a healthy child. The lines of suffering, even the pockmarks, disappeared and the touch of a smile came upon her lips. She was beatified in 1980.

COMMENT: We like to think that our proposed holiness is thwarted by our situation. If only we could have more solitude, less opposition, better health. Kateri repeats the example of the saints: Holiness thrives on the cross, anywhere. Yet she did have what Christians—all people—need: the support of a community. She had a good mother, helpful priests, Christian friends. These were present in what we call primitive conditions, and blossomed in the age-old Christian triad of prayer, fasting and alms: union with God in Jesus and the Spirit, self-discipline and often suffering, and charity for her brothers and sisters.

QUOTE: Kateri said: "I am not my own; I have given myself to Jesus. He must be my only love. The state of helpless poverty that may befall me if I do not marry does not frighten me. All I need is a little food and a few pieces of clothing. With the work of my hands I shall always earn what is necessary and what is left over I'll give to my relatives and to the poor. If I should become sick and unable to work, then I shall be like the Lord on the cross. He will have mercy on me and help me, I am sure."

CHINA—A REVERIE

To better understand the culture of China, let us briefly look at its history especially the role that the Catholic Church played in it. Some tough missionaries had preached to the Mongols in Peking as early as the fourteenth century. But when these missionaries died, the Gospel was not heard again in China until the 1500s. The voyages of Spanish and Portuguese explorers had opened up trade with India, Sri Lanka, Indonesia, and Malaysia. Traveling with the European traders to these Eastern countries were Catholic missionaries. Francis Xavier preached in all these lands. He even began a Catholic community in Nagasaki, Japan, which lasted up to the present despite persecution and the executions of Jesuits and Japanese Christians in 1597. Although Xavier died before he was able to enter China, his fellow Jesuit, Matteo Ricci (1552-1610), worked in the Imperial court of China for years. Ricci gained entry through his knowledge of astronomy and other sciences. Once he became well known in royal circles, Ricci began slowly to talk about his religion. Gradually some converts were made, although the emperors of China never converted. Ricci spoke fluent Chinese and dressed as Chinese people did; he respected Chinese civilization and traditions and tried to show how Christianity complemented these traditions.

Ricci, one of the first Jesuits in China, was known as the founder of the China mission. Xu Guangqi (1562-1633), a very influential convert to Christianity, was a member of the Ming dynasty bureaucracy from Shanghai who rose to the rank of Imperial Grand Secretary and helped Ricci convince China's ruling class, the mandarins, that Christianity had something to offer the Chinese that their culture lacked, namely, Christian revelation that they were uniquely capable of receiving. My friend Liam Brockey wrote how the Jesuits learned Chinese since they were among the first Europeans in the modern era to study the Chinese language. Since their goal was to transmit a complex religious message into a sophisticated culture, they subjected themselves to years of study before attempting to evangelize. The first Jesuit to dedicate himself to studying Chinese was Michele Ruggieri (1543-1607), who acquired Mandarin laboriously by drawing pictures and having a Chinese tutor teach him the corresponding characters. His successor Ricci, however, was able to rely on texts printed for Chinese schoolboys. Later Jesuits would use similar methods, benefiting from the experiences of their confreres who developed the first Western language course for learning Chinese. This course included readings and writing classes with Chinese and European masters.

The difficulties of working in China and Japan were immense. Both countries had highly sophisticated cultures, in many ways far advanced of any in Europe. Accepting Christianity seemed to these Far Eastern people to be an acceptance of Western culture, which they looked upon as inferior to their own. And since the missionaries were involved with foreign governments that were clamoring for favorable trade agreements, the missionaries were seen as foreign agents. Indeed, the Spanish and Portuguese governments wanted the missionaries to be agents for them, in effect agents of colonial power. Thus both countries discouraged the activity of missionaries in their countries. So much so, that Japan closed its doors to foreign trade in the early 1600s and began persecuting Japanese converts who were considered disloyal to Japan. Japan was virtually closed to the world until 1851.

With the revolutions of the late eighteenth and early nineteenth centuries, missionary activity slowed down. However, during the papacy of Gregory XVI (1831-46) missions were once again inaugurated. The strongest emphasis was given to Asia and Africa. By 1890 there were 500,000 baptized Catholics in China and over 350 Chinese priests. Unfortunately, China was being torn apart by the various Western powers who were taking over areas of the country for their own use. The Western powers controlled the coastal regions, forcing harsh trade agreements on the Chinese emperors. Although there were devoted Christian converts, many of the Chinese people saw the missionaries as part of the colonial exploitation of their country, as indeed some were. Many priests had not learned the lessons of Matteo Ricci, that is, they did not adapt their European ways to those of the people they were serving. As a consequence, in the Boxer Rebellion and the Communist Revolution, Christian Churches were expelled as foreign and oppressive influences.

The Church's history in China continued to be stormy in the twentieth century. In 1900 the Boxer Rebellion raged through China. The Boxers were fierce nationalists who wanted to rid China of all foreigners and foreign influences. Indeed, for nearly a century China had been dominated by the French, British, Japanese, German, and American businesses that were backed up by the armed forces of these countries. These foreign powers were stripping China of its natural resources, giving little in return. The British supplied China with opium in return for products the British got at extremely low prices. Missionaries accompanied the foreign powers, and in some cases created "rice Christians"; that is, people who converted because the missionaries supplied them with rice, the staple food in Asia. The Boxers wanted to end the abuse of China. In the violent rebellion, five bishops, 150 priests and religious, and 30,000 Catholics were killed. The rebellion was eventually crushed by troops from the foreign governments that took Peking and overran pockets of resistance. Tragically, not having learned their lesson, the foreign powers imposed even harsher terms on China.

In 1912 a republic was declared in China; the emperor had been overthrown. Yet old patterns and customs die hard. Soon the president of the republic was acting like an emperor, with few improvements for the masses of peasant farmers. Unrest seethed in the countryside. Wealthy landowners still extorted huge taxes from the peasants and in famines, hundreds of thousands of peasants died of starvation or diseases related to it. In the midst of this turmoil the Church continued to open schools and hospitals. By 1926 there were six Chinese Bishops and nearly 2,000 Chinese priests. Nevertheless, the Communist party under Mao Tse-Tung had begun organizing the peasants to rebel.

There were brief periods of peace between the republic's armies and the Communist Red Army, so that they could fight the Japanese invaders. Even so, President Chiang Kai-Shek directed most of his energy in combating Mao. As a result, many Chinese sided with the Communist Party, at least they seemed to be fighting the foes of China. When the war with Japan ended, civil war began. In 1949, Mao Tse-Tung declared the creation of the People's Republic of China. At the time, there were four million Chinese Catholics. As was true in the Soviet takeovers in Europe, the Chinese imprisoned or expelled all foreign missionaries. The Churches were liquidated. Mao stressed the need for Chinese nationalism and the destruction of all that was foreign and corrupt. Catholics lost their lives or had to go underground. Today worship is permitted but a bishop appointed by Rome would be rejected. The Chinese government wants to control the Catholic Church in China and to do so government officials appoint church leaders.

So, gentle reader, you can see from this brief history of China that over the centuries, Christianity has attempted on several occasions to take root and flourish in China, but each time it met with very limited success. When foreign missionaries were expelled in the early 1950's, the prevalent opinion was that once more Christianity would almost disappear from China. What a surprise then, when in the early 1980's, the West discovered that the Christian faith not only had survived but was growing. Today in light of the collapse of the Soviet Union, the crisis in international communism, and the rapid socio-economical changes in China, some observers think that Chinese Christianity may well be on the verge of entering its "golden age." 'Maybe' is the key word, predictions about China have often been proven wrong. Nonetheless signs of a renewed opportunity for Christianity are certainly abundant and call for a cautious optimism. But as you suspect, it is almost impossible to generalize about China because of its vastness and diversity. It's more like a multicolored mosaic with the reds more pronounced in one area while the yellows or the blues may dominate in others. The same goes for the Catholic Church: the situation varies from place to place. It is not an exaggeration to say that everything you hear about the Church in China is true at some time and at some place; and not true at another time and in another place.

In 1979 I enjoyed a three week Elderhostel to China staying in Beijing. I remember vividly the "rush hours" to and from downtown Beijing by the workers, solid traffic of thousands and thousands of BICYCLES! We visited the grounds of the Chinese Philosophers, Confucius (551-470 BC), and heard a lecture on his ethics, filial piety, benevolence, justice, propriety, intelligence and fidelity, all of which were his cardinal virtues. We heard about the teachings of the Chinese sage Mencius who trained under a grandson of Confucius in the 4th century B.C. Mencius's central belief was the inherent goodness of human nature. We took a bus tour thru the countryside to the Yellow River and back. One day we traveled to and walked on the top of the "Great Wall of China."

I was asked to give a farewell speech to some of the officials of Beijing. Most of these officials were communists. I finished my little ten minute "speech" with this thought: China is now in the process of choosing either Jeffersonian Democracy or Marxist Communism to govern and rule its great country. As I said these words I looked into the eyes of the officials, some looked cold, some looked surprised and some looked thoughtful. This process is still going on as far as I can see, THE FINAL OUTCOME IS STILL NOT DECIDED.

What follows now are some isolated paragraphs that might be informative and of interest to you and, as such, could invite you to read more about China to see what the outcome of this process might be since it is still going on.

1. Most missionaries left China or were expelled in the early 1950's. Sweeping arrests against Chinese bishops, priests, sisters and laity really began in the fall of 1955. In 1958, a political organization called the Chinese Catholic Patriotic Association (CCPA) was formed. Its role was to serve as a bridge between the Church and the state. To prove its patriotism and commitment not to act contrary to the interests of the country, the Patriotic Association voted to sever all political and economic ties with the Vatican and to obey the pope only in matters pertaining to faith and Church law. There is certainly no doubt that the Chinese government was, and still is, trying to exercise a large measure of control over the Church. The CCPA began to ordain bishops but they were not recognized by the pope. Bishops, priests, sisters and lay people who refused to go along with the government and the Patriotic Association's stance were sent to jail and to labor camps.
2. With the onset of the Cultural Revolution in 1966, all public religious activities ceased and all Church properties were confiscated. Church buildings that were not demolished or badly damaged were converted

into factories or storehouses. The Red Guards used torture and beating to force Christians to give up their faith. The CCPA was suspended. Many religious leaders and Christians had to endure public struggle sessions and were sent to prison and labor camps to join those who in the first place had refused to adhere to the association. In 1976, the ten-year nightmare of the Cultural Revolution came to an end. Religious leaders, priests and sisters were set free and resumed their ministry while the ban on religious belief and practice was relaxed.

3. A further sign of a more benevolent attitude toward religion came in 1978 with the reappearance of representatives from the five recognized religions: Taoism, Buddhism, Catholicism, Protestantism, and Islam. This resulted in a meeting of the Chinese People's Political Consultive Conference. This consultive body has no political power but serves in a bridge-building function among the constituencies of the delegates, the communist party, and the government. The CCPA resurfaced and since 1979, has been instrumental in the return of church properties to their former religious purposes. In 1982, China's new Constitution dropped the ultra leftist content of the preceding ones and recognized the freedom of religious belief for all Chinese people. The government became wary of the popular interest in Christianity and the substantial increase in church attendance. It was also worried by the resilience of the Catholic and Protestant underground composed of Christians who refused to submit to the control of the CCPA. Even with the reopening of China to the West, religious activities of foreigners within China have remained strictly controlled which made it difficult for foreigners to contact underground communities and further curtail the communities influence in government-approved religious bodies.

4. The Roman Catholic Church in China is not one Church but two Churches; one is faithful to Rome and the other is not, it is certainly a wounded and divided Church. There has never been a schism within that Church. In fact there are more and more hopeful signs that healing and reconciliation between the different segments are in the making; however the reality of the Roman Catholic Church in China remains complex and is still evolving.

5. In 1999 repressive measures against not officially registered Catholic communities have greatly increased. The underground Church has also been the target of mounting pressure from the government. Several priests and bishops remain in prison or have had their activities curtailed. Many underground Catholics play a prophetic role by their refusal to participate in a government-sanctioned organization. They dare to challenge the government policy regarding human rights and freedom of religion from a Catholic standpoint.

6. Pope John Paul II made repeated pleas to the Catholics of China to display toward one another "a love which consists of understanding, respect, forbearance, forgiveness and reconciliation." In many ways a complete normalization of diplomatic relations between China and the Vatican cannot happen unless reconciliation first occurs within the Chinese Catholic Church itself. In late 1999, the news spread that both sides had made substantial progress toward breaching the gap between Beijing's demand for a total and complete independence of the Chinese Church and Rome's insistence on an autonomous Chinese Church in communion with the pope and the universal Church. But during the course of the year 2000, two events (1)the ordinations of bishops without papal mandate on January 6 and 25, and (2)Rome's canonization of 120 Chinese martyrs on October 1, have seriously undermined the process. These misunderstandings point to the distance that still separates the Holy See and the Chinese government.

The present policy of the Chinese government to keep control over religious should not surprise us. After all, since the third century BC, Chinese emperors have always taken an active interest in regulating religions. As for outside organizations that propagate a confrontational and adversarial position on the situation of the Chinese Church, they are in direct defiance of the late John Paul II's plea for understanding, forgiveness, reconciliation and unity among Chinese Catholics. The Chinese Catholic Church today is quite different even from what it was in the 1980's when it emerged from long years of repression. It is growing in numbers, enjoying relative freedom of worship, and experiencing a renewal of vocations to the priesthood and religious life. But how many Catholic people are we talking about? The Catholic Church population is estimated at 12 million plus, but percentage wise this is only one percent of the population. Factors behind this slow growth are complex and many, some you have just read about, but one is certainly the bitter inner dispute that has just begun to fade away. Some other constraining realities:

1. Chinese Church issues: reconciliation within itself and with Rome.
2. Political issues of the relationship between the Chinese government, the Chinese Church and the Vatican.
3. Social issues: Religious freedom as linked to freedom of thought and expression.

At the same time Chinese society is also undergoing profound social and economic changes. This transformation is confronting the church with new issues and challenges as it begins to fulfill a meaningful role for various segments of the society. But most important is its continual battle for good against the evil of communism.

China today is a big violator of human rights and religious freedom. China today is practicing female infanticide with the result that there are four boys for every girl. That could make quite an army. China allows only one child per family. It is believed that China is making alliances with nations not too friendly to our country. So we better beware of any evil government. Also let us continue to lead the good people of China against the evil of its communist government.

Let us read two letters of missionary groups and what they are doing in China. The first letter from the Jesuits on December 2006:

Dear Sir/Madam,

Provincial Edward Schmidt, S.J. recently traveled to China. These are Fr. Schmidt's thoughts on the ministries he visited and the future of the Jesuits in China:

The purpose of this trip was to explain this huge, distant country which is expanding so rapidly and where church realities are sometimes hard to understand. China is one of Father General's five apostolic preferences for the whole society, and the Jesuits of China are hosting groups of provincials to make them acquainted with possibilities there.

The Beijing Center highlights the historic work of early Jesuits but also brings that work into the present by being an educational bridge between East and West. The Center works with most of the U.S. colleges and universities in providing year-long study programs to learn the language, culture, and opportunities to live and work in China today.

Jesuits have been involved in China since the late 1500s. Among the pioneers was the Italian Matteo Ricci who gained the confidence of Mandarin-Class Chinese and access to the imperial court. Successive generations of Jesuits in China contributed through mathematics, astronomy, and the arts to introduce the West to China and China to the West.

The ever-growing presence of Chinese people and Chinese products in all parts of the world is going to facilitate our learning.

Eileen Fitzpatrick
Director of Development
Chicago Province

Albert A. Hoffman, Jr.

The second letter (June 7, 2007) from the Columban Fathers, Missionary Society of St. Columban, PO Box 10, St. Columbans, NE 68056:

Dear Sir/Madam,

In the last few years, Columban missionaries have arrived at a transition in our work. Countries such as Korea, Japan and the Philippines now have a thriving Catholic church that is staffed by their own priests.

Our hope now is to focus on Pakistan and Mainland China. Pakistan is a Muslim nation, and the few Christians who live there in dire poverty are on the lowest rungs of the social ladder.

Mainland China's total control of the Catholic Church will not allow foreign missionaries to evangelize or run parishes. But the government permits foreign priests to teach in colleges and universities.

At this time, we have ten Columbans in China teaching subjects such as literature and philosophy.

Missionaries bring the Gospel and the sacraments to the world. In this they follow Jesus' call, "Go out to the whole world and preach the Good News." As far as Pakistan and China is concerned, talking about God is the first step.

What the future holds, we don't know. But we have Jesus' words that He'll be with us until the end of the world. Echoing His words, it seems that this generation of missionaries will sow the word, and the future ones will reap.

We will deep you and your loved ones in our Masses and prayers.

Well, what can we here at R.R.C. do to help the missionaries and the Church in its battle against evil? We can lift up our minds and hearts to Mary and her Son, Jesus Christ, the Prince of Peace. Each one of us can go to our room, close the door, and pray to our Father who is unseen. And your Father, who sees what you do in private, will reward you. Each one of us can fast without letting anyone else know we are fasting; only your Father, who is unseen, will know. And your Father, who sees what you do in private, will reward you. Each one of us can give alms thereby storing up riches for ourselves in heaven, where moths and rust cannot destroy, and robbers cannot break in and steal. For your heart will always be where your riches are. Remember your faith is your personal relationship with God and your personal relationship with your neighbor.

> Only the humble are grateful
> Only the grateful are happy
> Therefore only the humble are happy.

"Jesus, meek and humble of heart, make my heart like unto thine."

Prayer for Missionaries

Lord Jesus Christ, watch over your missionaries-priests, religious, and lay people-who leave everything to give testimony to Your word and Your love. In difficult moments sustain their energies, comfort their hearts, and crown their work with spiritual achievements. Let the ADORABLE image of You crucified on the cross, which accompanies them throughout life, speak to them of heroism, generosity, love, and peace.

Ah, gentle reader, let us conclude this reverie with a little more information on the canonization of 120 Chinese martyrs by John Paul II on October 1, 2000. Their feast day will be remembered every year on July 9th under the name of St. Augustine Zhao Rong, priest, and his companions. These 120 Chinese martyrs died between 1648 and 1930. Most of them (87) were born in China and were children, parents, catechists or laborers, ranging from nine years of age to 72. This group includes four Chinese diocesan priests. They were canonized by Pope John Paul II in 2000.

The 19th century was a time of Christian persecution in China. Imperial edicts imposed the death penalty for evangelization, as well as for the education and ordination of priests. Father Augustine Zhao Rong (1746-1815) was a Chinese diocesan priest who had been a soldier. While escorting French missionary Bishop Dufresse (also martyred in 1815), he learned of Christianity and was soon converted. He then became a priest and worked tirelessly to spread Christianity. In 1815, he was arrested and died in prison.

May these holy martyrs continue
To bring hope and grace
To Chinese Catholics

Bert Hoffman

ADDENDUM TO CHINA—A REVERIE

In the August issue of our RRC monthly in-house publication, The Phoenix, three of our people wrote excellent articles concerning China and should be of interest and value in understanding China.

(1.) Written by our Chaplin Larry Valentine:
Continuing our celebration of different countries and cultures, we worshipped at Mass celebrated in Chinese by the Reverend Dong Ping Francis Li on August 14, 2007.

Father Li is from the Diocese of Beijing, China, he grew up in a small village of Catholics near the capital and studied theology at

Mundelein Seminary. He is currently pursuing further studies. Father Li's celebration of Mass flowed seamlessly from Chinese to English and back again. His remarks sketched the history of Christianity in China from the 7th Century to the present situation of "one church with two sides." (see next article for details). Given the immense demographic and economic dominance of China, he urged us to pray, especially to Our Blessed Mother, for the growth of the faith in that great land.

2. The Uphill Journey of Catholicism in China (National Catholic Report article by John L. Allen, August 2007 condensed by RRC resident Mary Jane Coogan in observance of August as China Month)

With a population of 1.3 billion, China is trying to fill a void left by the collapse of economic communism. There are many wounded, helpless souls that are desperate to find something to believe in and to hold onto after these drastic changes.

There are many spiritual options in China, but three basic religious options are Muslim, Christian Pentecostal and Catholic. In northwestern China 20 to 30 million Muslims are in the grip of a revival funded largely by Saudi Arabia. Perhaps the most remarkable burst of energy is in China's Pentecostal Christian population. There are 111 million Christians in China, roughly 90% Protestant and mostly Pentecostal. By 2050 there will be 218 million Christians in China. There are 10,000 conversions to Christianity every day in China.

Curiously this booming "soul market" seems largely to have bypassed the Catholic Church with its mere 12 million members. There are four explanations for this: 1.) priest shortage and many Bishops either imprisoned or severally restricted. 2.) the rural face of Catholicism hampering urban expansion where Vatican II reforms would take root 3.) a Church deeply lacerated over the question of cooperation with the communist regime. For the most part, China watchers say Catholics who tolerate state oversight of their church as the lesser of two evils as the best survival strategy. Nonetheless, Catholics who reject this option out of unwavering loyalty to the Pope, and who often endure prison, harassment and discrimination, frequently regard "open" Catholics as compromised. 4.) Much Catholic conversation about evangelization in China is usually phrased as follows: "If China were to open up religious freedom . . .", or "If the Holy See and China were to establish diplomatic relations . . ." Pentecostal talk about mission, on the other hand, is very much phrased in the simple present. Most Pentecostals are not waiting for reform before carrying out aggressive evangelization programs such as bringing the Gospel message even into the Muslim world.

How things shake out religiously is of tremendously strategic importance. If Christianity ends up at around 20% of the population, China would become a more democratic, rule-oriented, basically pro western society such as South Korea. On the other hand, if dynamic Muslim movements create an Islamic enclave, western China could become a wealthier and more influential type of Afghanistan. Inter religious rivalry could destabilize this superpower and lead to global conflict. Catholicism could potentially offer a positive ingredient in China's new spiritual stew. A dynamic and growing Catholicism could be an important force in building a healthy civil society in China.

One key to Pentecostalism's worldwide expansion, however, is that Pentecostals live in constant expectation of just such a series of miracles. Perhaps rather than waiting for the "one step forward, two steps back" ballet between Rome and Beijing to reach conclusion, Chinese Catholics will steal a page from the Pentecostal's playbook, and embrace a vision of the "future is now."

3. MY HONG KONG TRIP
    By Mayme Biersner

January 1, 1997, LaVerne Hagglund and I were in Hong Kong to celebrate the last British New Year. The words Hong Kong translate as "Fragrant Harbor." We wanted to see this interesting city again to celebrate the Chinese New Year-the year of the RABBIT! We traveled as part of a tour group of 14 people.

It was an exciting experience for me-and I saw many changes. Arrival was at the gateway to Hong Kong, the new international Airport (Chek Lap Kok)-just completed and a marvel in itself.

Our tour guide was David Lau. He has eight sisters and brothers. They grew up living in housing best described as a "tent". Every time there was a typhoon or high wind, their home was destroyed. He was able to go to high school, then started as a bell boy, working up the scale to where he now is a Tour Conductor.

Hong Kong has experienced many changes since the British turned over the administration of the Island to the Chinese. The year 1997 was not easy, the economy went through difficult times and many people were laid off. The economy is recovering, and everywhere one can see new construction. However, day-to-day life in Hong Kong is apt to be much as before, especially on the back streets, where small businesses thrive, laundry hangs from windows, outdoor market stalls serve noodles, and incense from tiny makeshift altars curls into the air. Ordinary citizens will continue to work hard and invest their earnings, sweep their ancestors' graves on special holidays, and hope their children grow up to be prosperous.

One day I went to Lantau Island, one-hour by ferry on the South China Sea. It is almost twice the size of Hong Kong Island and is very mountainous. We left the bus and walked through an ancient fishing village. Back on the bus we continued through other villages, some being developed as commuter suburbs of Hong Kong. We went to Polin Monastery, home of a giant Buddha, Tai-O, (12 stories high), and Tung Chung, which has a Sung dynasty fort. There is also a Trappist monastery near Nim Shue Wan.

The food caused no discomfort to any of the members of our group. I made sure to visit the famous Peninsula Hotel for a delicious luncheon. One evening we splurged and had dinner at the Regent Hotel, named by some travel agents as the best hotel in the world.

Shopping is a delight: quality is high, and one can find almost anything in any price range one wants to pay. Cashmere sweaters, jade, eyeglasses, designer goods, all considerably less than one pays here. However, for women there was one problem: no shoes over size 7.

My reason for going, the New Year celebration itself, was spectacular. First a two-hour parade which included groups from around the world: Singapore, Australia, the Canadian Royal mounted Police, the Harlem Dance Troupe, Mexico, Scotland, etc.

The next night the fireworks display was also wonderful-held in Victoria Harbor. We were invited to a party atop a hotel to view the display. We were served champagne, along with an array of delicious food.

It is easy to get around on the island. There is a very good subway system, or the Star Ferry takes one from Kowloon Island over to Hong Kong in 15 minutes. For seniors the ferry ride is *free*.

Buddhism, Taoism, ancestor worship, Christianity, and animism are the major religions, and you'll see signs of them everywhere. The distinctions between religions are often blurred because Chinese people tend to be eclectic in their beliefs. It is not uncommon for the same Hong Kong citizen to put out food and incense for his departed ancestors at Spring Festival time, invite a Taoist priest to his home to exorcise unhappy ghosts, pray in a Buddhist temple for fertility, and take communion in a Christian church.

The Chinese, like westerners, have their own calendar and signs of the zodiac. As mentioned earlier, this is now the year of the Rabbit. The legend about this sign says, the Rabbit is born under the signs of virtue and prudence. The rabbit is honest, respected by all, and has a high degree of integrity. Graceful and sensitive, the Rabbit loves peace and easily hops away from trouble. If you were born in 1915, 1927, 1939, or 1951, you were born under the sign of the Rabbit.

The Chinese believe this to be an auspicious sign, indicating prosperity and plenty. Let us hope this sign also indicates peace and prosperity for all.

BRAZIL—A REVERIE

The territory of Brazil has been inhabited for at least 8000 years. The origins of the first Brazilians, who were called "Indians" by the Portuguese, are still a matter of dispute among archaeologists. The traditional view is that they were part of the first wave of migrant hunters who came into the Americas from Siberia across the Bering Strait. The Andes and the mountain ranges of northern South America created a rather sharp cultural boundary between the settled Agrarian civilizations of the west coast (which gave rise to urbanized city-states and the immense Inca Empire) and the semi-nomadic tribes of the east, who never developed written records before 1500. Archaeological remains (mainly pottery) indicate a complex pattern of regional cultural developments, internal migrations, and occasional large state-like federations. By the time the first European explorers arrived, all parts of the territory were inhabited by semi-nomadic Indian tribes, who subsisted on a combination of hunting, fishing, gathering, and agriculture.

It is generally accepted that Brazil was first discovered by Europeans on April 22, 1500 by PEDRO ALVARES CABRAL. Until 1530 Portugal had little interest in Brazil, mainly due to the high profits gained through commerce with Indochina. Portuguese Crown devised a system to effectively occupy Brazil. Through the Hereditary Captaincies system, Brazil was divided into strips of land that were donated to Portuguese noblemen, who were in turn responsible for the occupation of the land and answered to the king. Unfortunately, powerful land-owners claimed this land was given to them in perpetuity. In the first century after its European discovery, the country's major export, giving its name to Brazil, was brazilwood, a large tree whose trunk contains a prized red dye, and which was nearly wiped out as a result of over exploitation. Starting in the 17th century, sugarcane culture, grown in plantation's property called "engenhos" (factories) along the northeast coast. It became the base of Brazilian economy and society, because the use of black slaves in large farms to make sugar production for export to Europe. At first, settlers tried to enslave the Indians as labor to work the fields. However the Indians were found to be unsuitable as slaves, and so the Portuguese land owners turned to Africa, from which they imported millions of slaves. Africans became a substantial section of Brazilian population, and long before the end of slavery (1888) they had begun to merge with the European Brazilian population through miscegenation and mulatto work rights. During the first two centuries of the colonial period, attracted by the vast natural resources and untapped land, other European powers tried to establish colonies in several parts of Brazilian territory in defiance of the papal bull and the Treaty of Tordesillas which had divided the New World into two parts between Portugal and Spain. French and Dutch colonists tried to establish colonies but were unsuccessful in Rio de Janeiro (1555 to 1567) and in Salvador (1630 to 1654). Little French or Dutch cultural and ethnic influences remained of these failed attempts. Incidentally, that division of the New World in 1494 eventually became known as the DEMARCATION LINE, a meridian three hundred and seventy leagues west of the Cape Verde Islands, finally approved by the Pope in 1506. If perchance, gentle reader, you wish to read more about the history of Brazil, visit any library for resource history books covering the Empire of Brazil, the OLD REPUBLIC (1889-1930), Populism and development (1930-1964), Military Dictatorship (1964-85). Brazil's most severe problem today is arguably its highly unequal distribution of wealth and income, one of the most extreme in the world. By the 1990's, more than one out of four Brazilians continued to survive on less than one dollar a day. These socio-economic contradictions helped elect LUIZ INACIO LULA DA SILVA in 2002. After taking office, he used some conservative economic policies, warning that social reforms would take years and that Brazil had no alternative but to extend fiscal austerity policies. Lula has given a substantial increase to the minimum wage (raising from $200 to R$350 in four years). Lula also spearheaded legislation to drastically cut retirement benefits for public servants. His primary significant social initiative was the ZERO HUNGER program, designed to give each Brazilian three meals a day. Lula was re-elected President in the general 2006 election.

 Let us now trace the history of Roman Catholicism in Brazil. Brazil's strong Roman Catholic heritage can be traced to the Iberian missionary zeal, with the fifteenth-century goal of spreading Christianity to the infidels. In the New World, these included both Amerindians and African slaves. In addition to conversion, there were also strong efforts to enforce compliance with Roman Catholicism, including the Inquisition, which was not established formally in Brazil but nonetheless functioned widely in the colonies. In the late nineteenth century, the original Roman Catholic populace of Iberian origin was reinforced by a large number of Italian Catholics who immigrated to Brazil, as well as some Polish and German Catholic immigrants.

 According to all the constitutions of the republican period, there is no state or official religion. In practice, however, separation of church and state is weak. Government officials generally avoid taking action that may offend the church.

Brazil is said to be the largest Roman Catholic country in the world. In 1996 about 76 percent of the population, or about 122 million people, declared Roman Catholicism as their religion, as compared with 89 percent in 1980. The decline may have resulted from a combination of a real loss of influence and a tendency to be more objective in answering census questions about religion.

As in most dominant religions, there is some distance between nominal and practicing Catholics. Brazilians usually are baptized and married in the Roman Catholic Church. However, according to the CNBB (National Conference of Brazilian Bishops), only 20 percent of nominal Catholics attend Mass and participate in church activities, but the figure may be as low as 10 percent. Women attend Mass more often than men, and the elderly are more active in church than the young. In the 1990s, charismatic forms of Catholicism used unconventional approaches, along the line of those used by Pentecostal Protestant groups, to attempt revitalization and increase active participation.

Popular or traditional forms of Catholicism are widespread in the interior of the country. Many Brazilians pray to figures such as Padre Cicero (a revered priest who lived in Ceara' from 1844 to 1934), make pilgrimages to the site of the appearance of Brazil's patron saint, Our Lady of the Appearance (Nossa Senhora Aparecida), and participate in traditional popular rites and festivities, such as the Cirio in Bel'm and the Festa do Divino in central Brazel. Some use expressions of religious origin, such as asking for a blessing on meeting someone older or responding "God willing" when someone says "See you tomorrow."

During the 1970s, the progressive wing of the church made an "option for the poor." They were influenced by the doctrine of liberation theology, in which Brazilian theologians, such as Leonardo Boff, played a leading role, and followed the decision of Latin American Bishops' Conference in Medellin, Colombia, in 1968. The church organized Ecclesiastical Base Communities throughout the country to work for social and political causes at the local level. During the military regime, the progressive clergy managed to make the church practically the only legitimate focus of resistance and defense of human rights. In the early 1990s, conservative forces, supported by Pope John Paul II, gained power in the church.

Brazil is the largest of the Latin American countries, covering nearly half of the continent of South America, and is the fifth largest country in the world. The Atlantic Ocean extends along the entire eastern side of the country, boasting a coastline of 4,578 miles. The Brazilians, 169 million strong, and as you just ready a multi-ethnic mix of people and have a reputation of being very welcoming and hospitable. So, I thought the best way to capture the essence and flavor of Brazil would be through the eyes of the people who live there. So, I signed up for a three week ELDERHOSTEL in NOVEMBER, 1991 and did find the

Brazilians very friendly and kind living in a country of incredible beauty and passion. There were 15 people in our group, my favorite couple were Pat and Pamela Scott from Canada. Whatever the guide told us to do, Pat would do just the opposite, but a great guy. We spent one week in MANAUS, one week in SALVADOR, and one week in RIO DE JANEIRO. What follows now, Gentle Readers, are some of what we saw and did during these three weeks.

Manaus is the Capital of the state of Amazonas, and is the gateway to exploring the Amazon River basin. Started as a small trading post, MANAUS grew once demand for rubber sky-rocketed in the 19th century. The rubber barons acquired land, built a plantation, imported slaves, became millionaires and built the city of MANAUS. We visited the Opera House and viewed the elegance of the interior—all very plush seats, gold and silver decorations throughout the house and beautiful statuary. Enrico Caruso sang at its gala opening. For many years the rubber barons brought in the outstanding stars of Opera for their 6 week opera season, it was the social highlight of the year. By the way, we all flew into the Manaus International Airport originally built by the barons way back when.

One morning after breakfast our whole group was bussed down to the bank of the Rio Negro where our own "African Queen" was moored. We had to climb over the side to get on board. We traveled about 35 miles downstream to land at a very rickety pier, again clumsily climbing over the side and following the pier about an eighth of a mile. We then climbed rickety steps about 30 feet off the ground to our jungle lodge. We saw hundreds of frisky monkeys. Unfortunately one of the ladies laid down her camera which then reflected the sun. In an instant a monkey came out of no where, grabbed her camera which was last seen high up a tree branch and incidentally reflected back the sun. It was gone forever. I wonder if the monkey ever learned how to take pictures? I doubt it. Later, we walked along a short catwalk to explore the grounds—we saw a trail of continuous red army ants about 4 inches wide, a spotted leopard about an eighth of a mile away, and many, many trees. We were in the Rain Forest of the Amazon Jungle! One night about 5 of us were sitting in the small bar of the lodge, when we noticed a hairy shadowy something slowly coming toward us. Suddenly, our waiter took off his shoe and smashed the 10 inch diameter TARANTULA! The native waiter tried to assure us its bite would not kill us. Hmmm, his bite was supposed to only cause tarantism. What's that! It's a nervous AFFECTION characterized by melancholy, stupor, and an uncontrollable desire to dance. I guess that's not too bad. Well, its bad effect eventually did lead to the tarantella, a lively, passionate Neapolitan folk dance in 6/8 time, and a social dance evolved from it. Hmmm! But wait, our jungle experience doesn't end here. In the rivers of South America there is a small 2-inch long fish which is very voracious, attacking men and large animals that enter the water and inflecting dangerous wounds. Yes, you guessed it, the Piranha! One morning, some of us went Piranha fishing. Our guide told us under no circumstances bait the hook or attempt to remove the Piranha from the hook. We all caught Piranhas and closely followed our guides instructions, yes, all but one, PAT SCOTT! He shook the hooked Piranha, it fell to the bottom of the boat, Pat reached down to pick it up and screamed in pain—the Piranha had bit the end of his index finger all the way down to the bone! The guide rushed to him, his wife, Pamela, showed no compassion. We reeled in our lines and returned to the lodge where Pat received medical treatment. We returned to our hotel in Manaus the next day. That afternoon, our group flew to Salvador, BAHIA.

SALVADOR, the capital of BAHIA, pulses with its African rhythms, and is soothed with its salty breezes. We visited the historic CIDADE BAIXA and CIDADE ALTA with their colorful neighborhoods, in the distance we saw the famous lighthouse at the mouth of the bay. One morning we drove to a Sugar Cane Plantation. It was maintained as it was in the days when "Sugar Cane was King" of the Brazilian economy. There is no need to talk about plantation life since we all have seen movies of the South before the Civil War when "Cotton was King" of their economy. These movies were true and honest representations of plantation living. Some of you might have read Uncle Tom's Cabin by Harriet Beecher Stowe. The Chicago Historical Museum has an excellent exhibit on slavery and the cotton economy in the South before the Civil War.

We had a series of lectures given to us by an African Brazilian Voodoo practioner, it was quite an eye-opener for all of us!

Voodoo is a name attributed to a traditionally West African spiritual system of faith and ritual practices. Like most faith systems, the core functions of Voodoo are to explain the forces of the universe, influence those forces, and influence human behavior. Voodoo's oral tradition of faith stories carries genealogy, history and fables to succeeding generations. Adherents honor deities and venerate ancient and recent ancestors. This faith system is widespread across groups in West Africa. Diaspora spread Voodoo to North and South America, the Caribbean and the Philippines.

Because the Voodoo deities are born to each African clan-group, and its clergy is central to maintaining the moral, social, and political order and ancestral foundation of its villagers, it proved to be impossible to eradicate the religion. Though permitted by Haiti's 1987 constitution, which recognizes religious equality, many books and films have sensationalized voodoo as black magic based on animal and human sacrifices to summon zombies and evil spirits. Today in West Africa, the Voodoo religion is estimated to be practiced by over 30 million people! The word Voodoo is primarily used to describe the AFRO-CREOLE tradition of New Orleans. The versions of Voodoo which survived in the Southeastern United States were connected with Christian mysticism in the minds of rural African Americans. Segregation minimized the number of bi-lingual African Americans and at the same time minimized the number of whites who could translate voodoo writings to discover VOODOO in the spoken, sung, or written words of middle class, working class or working-poor African Americans and African Brazilians. Scholars debate the variations of VOODOO, how they have survived, how much they have changed, and to what extent Christianity in general or Catholicism in particular were used as covers to enable the survival of Voodoo. A common saying is that Haiti is 80% Roman Catholic, 20% Protestant, and 100% VOODOO. Thus the Catholic contribution to Haitian Voodoo is quite noticeable.

Public relations-wise, Voodoo has come to be associated in the popular mind with the lore about Satanism, zombies and "voodoo dolls." While there is evidence of zombie creation, it is a minor phenomenon in some rural cultures and not a part of the Voodoo religion as such.

The practice of sticking pins in dolls has history in European folk magic, but its exact origins are unclear. How it became known as a method of cursing an individual by some followers of what has come to be called New Orleans Voodoo is a mystery. Some speculate that it was used as a means of self defense to intimidate superstitious slave owners. Such voodoo dolls are not a feature of Haitian or Brazilian voodoo, although dolls intended for tourists may be found in many countries. The practice became closely associated with the Voodoo religions in the public mind through the vehicle of horror movies and popular novels. There is a practice in voodooism of nailing crude puppets with a discarded shoe on trees near the cemetery to act as messengers to the otherworld and portrayed as being used by voodoo worshippers in popular media and imagination for purposes of sympathetic magic toward another person. Another use of dolls in authentic Voodoo practice is the incorporation of plastic doll babies in altars and objects used to represent or honor the spirits.

Although VOODOO is often associated with Satanism, Satan is primarily our Abrahamic figure and has not been incorporated in Voodoo tradition. When Mississippi Delta folksongs mix references to Voodoo and to Satan, what is being expressed is social pain such as from racism, which is couched in Christian terms and blamed on the devil. Those who practice voodoo do not worship or invoke the blessings of a devil. From here we flew to RIO DE JANEIRO.

The second day of our week in RIO we were driven through the TIJUCA NATIONAL PARK to the top of the CORCOVADO MOUNTAIN (Hunchback Mountain). We walked from the parking lot around to the front of the mountain, looked up and saw for the first time the statue of Christ The Redeemer (CRISTO REDENTER). I immediately fell down on my knees, I was filled with the Fear of the Lord. Seeing this white Statue of the Lord with the endless blue sky above Him, here and there some white clouds brought to my mind how His second coming might be at the end of the world. The statue is 98 feet tall and the arms perfectly horizontal are 91 feet from finger tip to finger tip with the outer layers of the immense statue made of White SOAPSTONE imported from

Limhann, Sweden. The original design was done by a Brazilian named HEITOR DA SILVA COSTA. He was also the engineer in charge of its construction. He shared the project with French sculptor PAUL LANDOWSKI. It was built from 1926 to 1931. The statue weighs 1000 tons and was financed by donations which came mostly from Brazilian Catholics. The monument was inaugurated on the day of Our Lady of APARECIDA, 12 October 1931 by then president GETULIO VARGAS and Cardinal DOM SEBASTIAO LEME. It is one of the most worldwide symbols of the city, represents Jesus standing with outstretched welcoming arms. It is truly one of the Seven Modern Wonders of the World!

From the statue we beheld superb views of SUGAR LOAF MOUNTAIN, downtown Rio de Janeiro and Rio's beaches. Later in the week we would unfortunately find out that "all that glitters is not gold," when we visited the beaches and the city.

Sugarloaf Mountain is a peak situated in RIO from the mouth of GUANABARA BAY on a peninsula that sticks out into the Atlantic Ocean. Rising 1300 feet above sea-level, its name is said to refer to its resemblance to the traditional shape of concentrated refined loaf sugar.

The mountain is only one of several monolithic "MORROS" of granite and quartz that rise straight from the water's edge around RIO. By the 17th century the Portuguese had established Sugar Cane plantations and sugar cane became the primary export and upon completion of the processing the finished product was packed into bread like loaves for shipment. Hence the name Sugar Loaf. Navigators for years would spot the imposing figure at the entrance to GUANABARA BAY and sail into the bay.

How beautiful the white sand of the COPACABANA and IPANEMA beaches looked from Christ the Redeemer. However, when we drove past the beach we noticed no one was swimming in the blue water or walking along the white sand beaches. Why not? We were told the pipes of the sewage disposal system broke down depositing raw sewage into the water contaminating the swimming areas. We were also told that the sand beaches could be contaminated with parasites that could enter your bare feet, work their way up to your stomach and attach themselves to your intestines. Remember this was 1991, I'm sure this condition was corrected early the next year.

The next day we toured the downtown area of Rio, seeing beautiful buildings, plush restaurants, and attractive night clubs. One night we went to a club and saw the floor show and the Brazilian "PASSIONATE" dancing. Our own Pat and Pamela Scott competed with our dancing guides, guess who won? But now back to our tour of Rio. Our tour took us to the outskirts of the city where we left the bus and walked through an area of concentrated poverty, where hundreds of the very poor lived, with no electricity, only one well of water for all of these people, their clothes were rags and very little available food for them. This condition still exists. What follows is a little more exposure of these Brazilian FAVELAS, REAL EVIL.

Brazil is one of the countries with the most inequality in terms of the gap that exists between the very wealthy and the extremely destitute. A huge portion of the population lives in poverty. According to the World Bank, "one-fifth of Brazil's 173 million people account for only 2.2 percent share of the national income. Brazil is second only to South Africa in a world ranking of income inequality." This in effect leaves millions of Brazilians with little influence, recourse or hopes to deal with their dire situation in society. In big cities such as Rio de Janeiro and Sao Paulo, a third of the population lives in the surrounding slums, and social conditions for the poor are terrible. In 2001, the country's official unemployment figure was 6.4% but, in the slums around the largest cities, employment is much worse and likely not fully recorded in government statistics.

The lack of educational opportunity for poor in Brazil only aggravates extreme inequality among the country's citizens. The poorest 25 percent in urban areas have completed less then four grades of schooling, while the wealthiest 25 percent have completed on average ten years of schooling. While people living in the slums frequently state that education would help give them the skills to get better jobs, they maintain that for them it is either a matter of working and having food to eat or going to school and starving. As one slum resident put it, "You have to choose between working and studying because you can't do both. And if you choose to study, what are you going to eat?"

In addition, according to the World Bank, the country has the world's highest murder and homicide rates, due mainly to drug-related violence in the slums. Brazilians living in slums claim that every day they have to deal with, "theft, vandalism, muggings, rapes, gang fights, murders, and organized crime." "People are very hostile here. They even have knife fights over soccer." "People get killed at parties and on their way to and from parties."

A recent article in the BBC news compared the situation in the slums surrounding Rio de Janeiro to a war zone. There are an estimated 5,000 to 6,000 armed children in Rio alone. Statistics also show that over the past 14 years guns killed a total of 4,000 children under the age of eighteen. Many claim that this happens because the authorities have abandoned the slums, making them similar to war zones where gangs and drugs rule the scene.

Perhaps what is most tragic about the violence and poverty in the slums of Brazil is the effect on the lives of children. It has been estimated that about 30 million children live in conditions that are subhuman and inadequate for their development. They also experience violence at the hands of authorities, and there are countless human rights violations regarding street children by police officers and other adults. "Violence against and by street children is a part of the fabric of life in which these victims and perpetrators dangerously live. Violence is an aspect of identity as tragically indelible as the scars that crisscross their bodies."

Indirect-or more or less direct-violence against street children in the slums can be gauged through the infant mortality and illiteracy rates, and in general the subhuman living conditions prevailing. The number of young children with arms or involved in gangs and drug trafficking, or simply the way that they use violence to get food and clothing, are concrete indications of the violence that breeds in such brutal socio-economic conditions.

A recent study by the International Labor Organization shows that crime by children related to drug abuse and trafficking in Rio has increased during the 1990's. Also, by the year 2000 the children's age of entry into drug trafficking and other related crimes fell from 15-16 to 12-13. Children involved in this type of violence share some characteristics. The study shows that they belong to the poorest families in the slums, and that they have less than the country average of 6.4 years of schooling. When asked what they thought the best solution to the problem was, slum residents responded that investment in education and generation of employment and income were the best.

Direct violence is not the only thing killing children. In the slums, hunger, malnutrition and disease are possibly even larger threats to the survival of these children. These deaths certainly weigh in on the mortality statistics; UNICEF reported that in 1993 over 226,000 Brazilians less than five years old died. In these conditions, it is not surprising that children grow up with little hope for survival or of improving their situation in life.

> "STREET CHILDREN ARE A REMINDER, LITERALLY ON THE DOORSTEPS OF RICH BRAZILIANS AND JUST OUTSIDE THE FIVE-STAR HOTELS WHERE THE DEVELOPMENT CONSULTANTS STAY, OF THE CONTRADICTIONS OF CONTEMPORARY SOCIAL LIFE: THE OPULENCE OF THE FEW AMID THE POVERTY OF THE MAJORITY, THE PLETHORA OF RESOURCES AMID THE SQUANDERING OF OPPORTUNITIES. THEY EMBODY THE FAILURE OF AN UNACKNOWLEDGED SOCIAL APRTHEID TO KEEP THE POOR OUT OF VIEW... THEY ARE PAINFUL REMINDERS OF THE DANGEROUS AND ENDANGERED WORLD IN WHICH WE LIVE."

From the day they are born children in the slums of Brazil are unable to live as children and must deal with surviving in a world where all of the cards appear to be stacked against them. The slums in many areas of Brazil have become such terrible places that the police are afraid to enter and authorities are thinking of isolating them with walls.

Achieving peace in such extremely violent settings is a very hard challenge that cannot be pursued without removing the root causes of poverty. These causes involve an economic and social system that is not producing jobs or providing education adequately, and that therefore presents itself as aggressive and violent to the downtrodden.

The International labor Organization study on children in Brazil proposed four policies to be implemented in order to deal with the issue of children and violence in the slums: generation of income and employment for families of children involved in drug trafficking, investment in education and social protection instruments; integrated actions in popular spaces embracing generation of income, leisure, education, urbanization, etc.; and measures in the legal field, such as discriminating between different drugs.

Brazilian President Luiz Inacio Lula da Silva promised to eliminate hunger by the year 2007 when he was elected, but hunger still affects the lives of too many Brazilians. There is no doubt that the attitude towards the problem has changed since the massive killings of 'overabundant' street children a decade or so ago. But recent data on Rio de Janeiro shows that 15% of the population lives below the poverty line of $27 a month. Because of this situation, "The conditions on the outskirts of big cities remain grim, with youths hanging around doing nothing, an explosion in violent crime and a severely deficient police and judicial system." A successful war on hunger that may allow for schooling, and better educational opportunities appears as the principal challenge for moving towards social peace.

Well, gentle reader this is as good a time as any to talk about the Missionaries in Central and South America. The missionaries who came to the colonies were usually powerless to stop the exploitation of the people. Nevertheless they preached the Gospel to the Indian peoples. The earliest missionaries were the Franciscans who began work on Santo Domingo in the Caribbean in 1500. In 1524 the Franciscans came to Mexico, later joined by the Dominicans and then the Augustinians. Generally they tried to learn the local languages, construct an alphabet, and then write catechisms. Mexico had its first bishop in 1530. Soon there were missionaries in Panama, Colombia, Ecuador, Guatemala, and Honduras. By 1549 the first Jesuits arrived in the jungles of Brazil, the colony owned by Portugal. Soon they fanned out into other parts of the continent, including Paraguay, Peru, and Mexico.

The Indians became Christians for a number of reasons. First, some of the missionaries were good to them. Some believed that the Christian god must be stronger than their gods because the Spaniards conquered them. Therefore, if they converted, they would be on the winning side-or at least they would have something in common with the Spaniards. No doubt others genuinely believed in the new faith. These reasons were similar to the ones the early GOTHS, VANDALS, and FRANKS had for converting not too many centuries before.

Inevitably, as in Asia, "Christian" became equivalent to "Spanish." In this very confusing situation the missionaries themselves ran into split loyalties. They were loyal Spaniards, but they wanted to serve the people. Thus odd practices occurred. For example, in most places the Christian Indians were not given Communion for many years; they were allowed only the sacraments of Baptism, Penance, and Matrimony, sacraments that they could understand more easily than Eucharist. By the same token, no Indians were ordained as priests for almost three hundred years because the king of Spain forbade it.

As in Asia, the Indians were also victims of abuses, the worst one being slavery. Again, the friars were their main defenders. Especially famous for confronting the abuses was BISHOP DE LAS CASAS; he was the main power that finally caused the king to prohibit slavery. He went to Colombia in 1545 and worked for Indian rights there, eventually being forced out by plantation owners. In Guatemala the Spaniards tried to capture him, but he managed to escape. Conditions were much the same in Honduras and Panama. Las Casas had many allies among the friars and the Jesuits.

In the 1600s in places such as Paraguay, the Jesuits set up towns and areas like reservations for Indians. Here the Indians could live together under Indian authority. The Jesuits set up schools, weaving projects, and communal farming. These settlements were so successful that the Jesuits made enemies among greedy colonizers. Eventually these enemies forced the Jesuits out of South America.

Pope Benedict XVI made a visit to Latin America (BRAZIL) May 9-14, 2007. The Pope identified a host of social and religious challenges and said the church should respond by focusing more clearly on the person of Jesus Christ. He said economic indicators give reason for hope, as do efforts to fight drug trafficking and corruption. He cited inroads by secularism, threats against the family and the institution of marriage, and an erosion of traditional Latin American values and said that in response the church needs to put greater emphasis on the religious education of its own members.

One big reason the evangelical sects have attracted Catholics, he told Brazilian bishops, is that many Catholics are insufficiently evangelized and their faith is weak, confused and easily shaken. In a country where televangelists have had great success with simple religious messages, he did not hold out any easy solutions. He said the church should conduct a methodical evangelization aimed at personal and communal fidelity to Christ. Firm doctrinal content is essential to faith formation and at nearly every of his stops he suggested wider use of the Catechism of the Catholic Church.

On May 14, Pope Benedict canonized Brazil's first native-born saint, Friar ANTONIO GALVAO, to the cheers of up to a million faithful from across Latin America who cheered and waved flags at the outdoor mass at Sao Paulo's Campo de Marte Airfield. The open-air Mass marked the highlight of the Pope's visit to Brazil, the largest Catholic country in the world. Saint GALVAO, who lived from

1739-1822, is one of the best-known religious figures in Brazil, renowned for his healing powers. Antonio Galvao was born in the town of GUARANTINGUETA, in what is now SAO PAULO state. His family was wealthy and well-respected. His father was a Portuguese immigrant and his mother claimed descent from a legendary explorer and emerald prospector. The young Galvao began his studies at a Jesuit seminary. But as the order came under persecution from mainstream religious leaders, Galvao was transferred by his father to a Franciscan school. He was ordained in 1762 and six years later, he became a preacher and confessor at the St. Francis Friary in Sao Paulo. Over the course of his career, Friar Galvao supervised the construction of many religious buildings. Sao Paulo remained the focus of his attentions. On his many journeys through the city, he is said to have avoided using horses or slaves for transport, choosing to visit people on foot. Friar Galvao's elevation to sainthood came after the Catholic Church said it had established that he had performed at least two miracles-including healing a young girl whom doctors had deemed incurable. Friar Galvao died at the Recolhimento da Luz monastery on 23 December 1822.

Pope Benedict XVI inaugurated the Fifth General Conference of the Bishops of Latin America and the Caribbean. Before leaving Brazil, he delivered an opening address to the 260 bishops present. He made several key points:

* The Church best contributes to solving social and political problems by promoting a moral consensus on fundamental values which must come before the construction of just social structures.
* Among Catholics, the bishops should give priority to Sunday Mass and faith formation of young people and adults.
* Both Marxism and capitalism have failed to deliver on their ideological promises to build a better world because they are systems divorced from individual morality. Along with his critique of capitalism and the growing rich-poor gap, the pope warned that globalization risks creating vast monopolies and treating profit as "the supreme value."
* The evangelization of the Americas was not the "imposition of a foreign culture," and any attempt to retrieve pre-Colombian indigenous religions would be "a step backward" for Latin Americans.

Ah, my gentle readers, how best to end this Reverie? After much thought and hoping you will use your imagination and study time to become aware of the continuing battle between GOOD and EVIL in today's world, read now the words of my good friend, George WEIGEL:

> "Latin America Catholicism, like Latin America itself, must become the protagonist, the subject, of its own history. For more than half a millennium, Latin America had thought of itself as the object

of history-made-elsewhere: first, the history made by the colonial power of Spain and Portugal; later, the history made by the giant beyond the Rio Grande, El Norte, the United States. This instinctive self-deprecation-this sense of being on the receiving end of history, rather than the forging end-has to stop. Latin America is a diverse, rich continent of cultures formed by the unique interaction of native, Iberian, and African peoples. It is a cornucopia of natural and human resources. Yet it never seems to be able to gather itself for civilizational greatness, in part, because of this ingrained habit of thinking of itself as a victim. If Pope Benedict manages to ignite the idea that Latin America must take charge of their own history, which means, among other things, confronting the shadow-side of that history, including the rampant corruption and statism that block economic and political progress throughout the continent today, he will have done Latin America a great favor.

May the bishops and theologians who have internalized the John Paul II Revolution carry the day in Brazil with the aid of Benedict XVI, who once reminded liberation theologians enamored of 'Marxist analysis that' that God wishes to be adored by people who are free."

Jesus said "I have come to set you free."

Bert Hoffman

GERMANY—A REVERIE

Part of Germany is, of course, Octoberfest!
Part of Octoberfest is eating, drinking and singing!
Part of one of Duetchland's happiest songs follows!
    In Munchen steht ein Hofbrauhaus
    Ein zwei suffa!
    Da lacut so manches tanchen aus
    Da hat so manchon brave man
    Und spact am ibend haert er auf
    So geht es im Hofbrauhaus!

Part of a student's translation now follows!
    In Munich there is a beer hall
    One, Two, Drink!
    Many barrels of beer are empty
    Many brave men have showed how much they can drink.
    Early in the morning he sets out drinking
    At the Hofbrauhaus!

Part of everyone's favorite singing and drinking toasts has to be!
    Ein Prosit, Ein Prosit, Gemuetlikeit
    Ein Prosit, Ein Prosit, Gemuetlikeit
    Eins, Zwei, Drei, Suffa!

My cousin, John Pontius, was a Chicago policeman and a member of the German American Police Association (GAPA). The association planned a three week trip to Germany for Octoer 1977 to celebrate the OCTOBERFEST. Each officer could bring members of his family, so John's wife, Kathy, his sister, Mary Lou, and myself joined the group bringing the total to 40 people. What a time we had! We arrived in MUNICH (MUNCHEN) for the opening day of the Octoberfest and followed the opening day procession with its many brass bands into the big beer tents and stalls with pretzels, cheeses, and sausages. Inside the tents were many long narrow tables with seats on both sides. There we sat singing, eating, and drinking while watching the entertainment of yodeling, dancers, and singing. Yes, there were buxom waitresses all in colorful costumes bringing 8 liters of cold bier to the tables, each hand holding 4 steins, each stein held one liter of beer, an awesome sight. We drank, ate, and sang for four hours. To hear all those people singing happy German songs, entwining their arms with the persons next to them and swaying back and forth to the beat of the ompah bands is a musical thrill never to be forgotten! The next day we staggered to the Ratzkeller for a luncheon with the Mayor of Munich who spoke perfect English. He eventually turned us over to the Chief-of-Police who gave us a tour of Police Headquarters. He also spoke perfect English. On the way there, he pointed out the new City Hall and we were on time to see and hear its famous GLOCKENSPIEL. Here are a few rememberances of our three weeks: The walled city of ROTHENBERG, its city square and gates to the city; Ludwig's Castle on the CHIEMSEE River; the inspiring Cathedral of Cologne; the surrounding district of the City of Rudesheim which can truthfully be called a wine paradise, in fact, every year 10 million gallons of delicious wines are produced. RUDESHEIM was a stop on our Rhine boat trip. After disembarking we strolled along tiered walkways to the highest part of the city, these walkways had beautiful outside cafes and shops. Yes, as we continued on our Rhine trip we did hear the seductive, soft, inviting song of the LORELEI ROCK, but we did not succumb to her invitation! We saw many ancient castles very high on the distant mountain slopes; we saw HEIDELBERG, that famous University town on the NECKAR RIVER, where we heard a student choir sing Romberg's and other love songs while we strolled along the very green paths of the campus (The Student Prince); we saw WEISBADEN, magical and attractive, where my cousin Bernie Pontius served in the air force as a corporal from 1946-47.

The Rhine is not merely a river, for it is also the mirror of the history of the Western Hemisphere. Its picturesque banks are graced with old towns with their fine cathedrals and churches and with ancient castles rich in legend high above the slopes of innumerable vineyards. Yes, all of you who were fortunate to travel over the Rhine sometime in your life can recall the loveliness of Rhine country which certainly must have left an indelible impression on your mind, a gift to you from God.

Hmmm, let us now continue our Reverie by reading a little about the very early history of Germany. The Germanic tribes, which probably originated from a mixture of peoples along the Baltic Sea coast, inhabited the northern part of the European continent by about 500 B.C. By 100 B.C., they had advanced into the central and southern areas of present-day Germany. At that time, there were three major tribal groups: the eastern Germanic peoples lived along the Oder and Vistula rivers; the northern Germanic peoples inhabited the southern part of present-day Scandinavia; and the western Germanic peoples inhabited the extreme south of Jutland and the area between the North Sea and the Elbe, Rhine, and Main rivers. The Rhine provided a temporary boundary between Germanic and Roman territory after the defeat of the Suevian tribe by Julius Caesar about 70 B.C. The threatening presence of warlike tribes beyond the Rhine prompted the Romans to pursue a campaign of expansion into Germanic territory. However, the defeat of the provincial governor Varus by Arminius at the Battle of the Teutoburg Forest in A.D. 9 halted Roman expansion; Arminius had learned the enemy's strategies during his military training in the Roman armies. This battle brought about the liberation of the greater part of Germany from Roman domination. The Rhine River was once again the boundary line until the Romans reoccupied territory on its eastern bank and built the Limes, a fortification 300 kilometers long, in the first century A.D.

The second through the sixth centuries was a period of change and destruction in which eastern and western Germanic tribes left their native lands and settled in newly acquired territories. This period of Germanic history, which later supplied material for heroic epics, included the downfall of the Roman Empire and resulted in a considerable expansion of habitable area for the Germanic peoples. However, with the exception of those kingdoms established by Franks and Anglo-Saxons, Germanic kingdoms founded in such other parts of Europe as Italy and Spain were of relatively short duration because they were assimilated by the native populations. The conquest of Roman Gaul by Frankish tribes in the late fifth century became a milestone of European history; it was the Franks who were to become the founders of a civilized German state.

Hmmm, the history of Germany from the late fifth century to the beginning of the sixteenth century is beyond the scope of this Reverie. But at the beginning of the sixteenth century everyone that mattered in the Western Church was crying out for reform. For a century or more Western Europe had sought for reform of the Church 'in head and members' and had failed to find it. If you asked people what they meant when they said that the Church was in need of reform, they would not have found it easy to agree. Gadzooks, was this a can of WORMS—again way beyond the scope of this Reverie. Permit me to jump directly to MARTIN LUTHER, professor of Holy Scripture at the University of WITTENBERG, who on All Saints' Eve, 31 October 1517, fastened to the door of the castle church at Wittenberg a placard inscribed with "Ninety-five Theses upon Indulgences'. He announced that he was ready to defend these theses at a public disputation. The Reformation had begun. Ah, gentle reader, if you are interested in pursuing this subject, a very good book, easy to read is THE REFORMATION by Owen Chadwick from PENGUIN BOOKS, The Penguin History of the Churches. But now, let us jump to the Peace of Augsburg in 1555 that is very relative to Germany.

The Peace of Augsburg brought peace but did not settle the religious disagreements in Germany. For one thing, its signatories did not recognize

Calvinism, a relatively stringent form of Protestantism that was gaining prominence around the time the Augsburg treaty was signed, in what has been called the Second Reformation. Adherents to both Calvinism and Lutheranism worked to spread their influence and gain converts in the face of the Counter-Reformation, the attempt of the Roman Catholic Church to regroup and reverse the spread of Protestantism. Followers of all three religions were at times successful, but only at the expense of the others.

Fear of religious subversion caused rulers to monitor the conduct of their subjects more closely. Attempting to help the modern reader understand the intensity and pervasiveness of this fear, Mary Fulbrook, a noted British historian of Germany, has likened it to the anxiety prevailing in the first years of the Cold War. An example of the social paranoia engendered by the religious tensions of the period is Protestant Germany's refusal until 1700 to accept the Gregorian calendar introduced by the papacy in 1582 because the reform entailed a one-time loss of the days between October 5 and 14. Many Protestants suspected that Roman Catholics were attempting somehow to steal this time for themselves.

By the first decades of the seventeenth century, religious controversy had become so obstructive that at times the Reichstag could not conduct business. In 1608, for example, Calvinists walked out of the body, preventing the levying of a tax to fight a war against the Turks. In the same year, the Evangelical Union was established by a few states and cities of the empire to defend the Protestant cause. In 1609 a number of Roman Catholic states countered by forming the Catholic League. Although both bodies were less concerned with a sectarian war than with the specific aims of their member states, their formation was an indication of how easily disputes could acquire a religious aspect.

So, again we gather a little more insight into the culture of Germany. Let us now shift our attention to the German immigrants to the United States and with this little background better understand their "modus operandi."

Except for the American Indians, all Americans are immigrants or the descendants of immigrants. During the colonial period, settlers came by the thousands. From the end of the American Revolution to today some 46 million people have migrated to our shores. From 1830 to 1860 five million immigrants came to America, most of these coming from Ireland and Germany. Germans who had migrated for economic reasons were joined, after the failure of the Revolution of 1848, by German liberals and intellectuals, who came to escape political persecution. Because the United States successfully absorbed different peoples and heritages to form an American nationality and culture, the United States has been called a "melting pot." Some outstanding German immigrants have been Governor John Peter Altgeld of Illinois; optical equipment manufacturers John J. Bausch and Henry Lamb; engineer and designer of the Brooklyn and St. Louis bridges, John Roebling; civil service reformer, Carl Schurz; electrical engineer Charles Steinmetz. In the vanguard of the German immigrants to America were the political refugees, liberals who had taken a part in the revolutions of 1848 only to lose out in the end before the forces of reaction. Some men of this type, Carl Schurz and Franz Sigel, for example, soon achieved a greater prominence in their adopted land than they had ever known in Germany. Still others left to avoid the compulsory military service required by most German princes, and others to get away from distressing economic conditions for which no remedy seemed available. The success of the English manufacturers with factory-made textiles brought ruin to the numerous German household producers of linen, while crop failures in the Rhine Valley and a losing struggle to hold the English grain market meant critical times for agriculture.

The average German immigrant had often saved enough money to get a start in the new land. Sometimes he went into business, and whole cities, such as Cincinnati, St. Louis, and Milwaukee, soon exhibited many of the characteristics qualities of the German. More frequently he bought a farm and, unaccustomed to the thriftless methods into which an abundance of rich soil had betrayed the Native Americans, he farmed carefully and prospered immediately. Now connect the above three cities with lines and you form what is known as the German Triangle. The majority of immigrants within and around this triangle were Germans, including the cities. Unlike the Irish, the Germans rarely settled in the East, but went instead to the Middle West, where lands were cheaper and opportunity more abundant. For a generation or more they continued to speak the German language, and they clung tenaciously to the manners and customs of their European homes. Great lovers of music and of good-fellowship, each German community was apt to have its LIEDERKRANZ, its TURNVEREIN, and its BIERGARDEN. In Wisconsin the German influence was so pronounced that there was talk of making the state over into an ideal German commonwealth.

Chicago in time would become the major city in this German Triangle. So to continue our Reverie on Germany, I want to quote the excellent brief history of Chicago that was written by my friend and historian ROBERT R. MORRIS for the 150th anniversary of St. Michaels Parish in his book entitled St. Michael's Parish, Chicago's legend, 1852-2002 "OLD TOWN." Incidentally my grandparents came from Germany and were pioneers in the building of St. Michael's church and schools, which both my parents attended. Following begins his article.

Before St. Michael's Parish came to be, in fact before any church came to be here, the area we know as Chicago was a mosquito-plagued swamp, and a smelly one at that. The south end of Lake Michigan ("Michi-kamma" in the Ojibwa language, meaning "It is a big lake") offered the casual visior mostly a collection of sand dunes, reed-filled bogs and wetlands.

It would have been a scenic vacation spot if it were not spoiled by the flies, mosquitoes and the gnats. And then, there was the mud; the slippery, frozen mud after the winter winds blew in. Besides, the wild onions added their own unmistakable aroma to the locale.

So Chikagu ("the smelly place") offered limited unique charms to the few locals and the occasional passersby. Who knew?

The French came here first. Father Pierre Marquette and his crony Louis Jolliet canoed through the area in 1673. But they didn't stay long since they were looking for a way to get to the Mississippi River because they were in a big hurry to get to New Orleans. The river that opened into the lake held great promise for them as a direct passage to the Gulf of Mexico, so on they paddled.

Twenty years after Marquette's visit, another Frenchman, Father Pierre-Francois Pinet came to town, intending to stay. He built the Guardian Angel Mission along the Chicago River in 1696. But conditions were brutal and the Indians weren't too keen on adopting the new religion, so in 1700, the 40-year-old Pinet abandoned Chicago's first Catholic church and moved on to downstate Cahokia where there were many more French traders and life a bit less perilous.

During the 1700s, the occasional trapper came along, however the area primarily belonged to the Potawatomie. The tribe didn't have long roots here either, since they originally broke off from the Ojibwa nation in Ontario, and settled in what is now western Lower Michigan about 500 years ago. However, a tribal dispute sent the Potawatomies packing off to the western shore of the big lake in the 1630s, just in time for the French to come calling.

Throughout the 1700s, the French and the Indians got along fairly well until the British came and stirred things up. Eventually the British declared war on the French, who despite a formidable alliance with the Indians lost the war—what we call today the French and Indian War in 1763. So, the French packed up their voyageurs and headed for Canada, leaving a power vacuum at the south end of Lake Michigan.

During the 1770s, Chicago's first full-time non-Indian resident, Jean Baptiste Point du Sable, a French-born Haitian, came to set up a trading post on the north side of the river. He stayed until the population swelled to a few dozen and left in 1800 for more open country in Missouri.

The North American adventures of both the French and British were but a sideshow, and the two nations then squared off in a bitter war in Europe. Distracted by the annoying French, the British were not paying close attention to the upstart American colonists, who also wanted to run their own show.

Frustrated by fate, the British capitulated and the American nation was born in 1783. The Lake Michigan region became part of the new Northwest Territories of the United States. In 1795, the Potawatomies ceded a tract of land at the mouth of the "Chicago" River to the U.S. Government.

The federal government eventually built Fort Dearborn in 1803 as a military outpost to govern the raw pioneer territory and protect the small but growing band of settlers who came and stayed despite the hardships.

Despite the hardships, Chicago's location was a winner and under the protection of the soldiers at the fort, a thriving community grew. There were bumps along the way, as an Indian uprising in 1812 resulted in a massacre of soldiers and settlers. But the fort, rebuilt in 1816, once again offered protection for those who chose to live and work at the south end of Lake Michigan.

Illinois became a state in 1818 and by 1837, Chicago's 250 residents voted to incorporate the community. Their livelihood was supported by the village's location as a fledgling shipping center for frontier goods. The lush swamp and glacial earth also made the region a marvelous place to farm, so the city also became a regional distribution point for locally grown produce.

By the late 1830s, the greatest fear of residents—Indians—was reduced as all Indian nations in the region, defeated in the Black Hawk War, relinquished their ancestral land claims and moved west. The settlement floodgates opened with a bang. By 1840, Chicago had 4,000 residents and the explosive growth had only begun.

At the middle of the 19th century, Chicago benefited from technology and war. The new railroads found Chicago to be a great crossing from east to west as countless lines snaked their way through the city. The Civil War turned Chicago into a munitions and supply manufacturing shipping location.

The growth of commerce in Chicago created a frenzy to fill the jobs in the many factories, plants and offices springing up around the expanding city. Employers filled those jobs with eager and willing new immigrants to the nation.

First the Irish came by the thousands, many to escape British domination, economic disaster and starvation in Ireland. But swiftly on their heels came the Germans, who fled increasing political unrest in the towns, hamlets and cities of the unstable city-states and principalities that did not yet form a cohesive country. By the 1840s, democratic revolutionary movements erupted in many of the German-speaking states; most of them were brutally crushed creating a flood of people who simply wanted to get out of harm's way.

During the great immigration waves, the new populations understandably moved into neighborhoods where other immigrants lived—to share language, culture, food, song—and faith.

The small but growing German community in Chicago settled primarily north of the Chicago River—on the outskirts of town really. By 1846, two Catholic Parishes served the German settlers, St. Peter and St. Joseph. However by the 1850s, the stream of immigrants grew and another parish was clearly needed.

One problem not immediately recognized by the Catholic hierarchy in Chicago at the time was the diversity and lack of unity of so many of the German immigrants. The church hierarchy and clergy in America were overwhelmingly Irish, who shared a fairly homogeneous political, cultural and religious background. But the Germans came from a place that was not yet an identifiable single country during the 1840s. They often had unique and individual regional dialects, customs, dress and outlooks. Simply establishing parishes to cater to German population faith "needs" was much more tricky than it appeared on the surface. This issue would haunt the German parishes and Irish hierarchy for years. Here ends this brilliant article written by Robert R. Morris.

As the German immigrants settled in Chicago, they moved into the area north of the Chicago River known today as "Old Town." Most of the dwellings and tenements were in the south part of the neighborhood. Newcomers with a farming background moved into the northern section, draining and taming the swamplands where they grew cabbage, potatoes, celery and other crops.

The population continued to grow and the faith needs of the community could no longer be easily served by the two existing German Catholic Churches in the diocese. Amidst the background of a discordant German immigrant population, combined with the exploding numbers of daily new arrivals, the bishop authorized the founding of St. Michael's Parish in 1852; however internal disagreements and a "revolving door" series of pastors (5 pastors from 1852-1860) cast doubt on whether the new faith community would come together and survive. By 1860, a change was essential for the parish to continue and flourish. Bishop Duggan turned to the Redemptorists for help. The Redemptorists had toiled for decades in the many German principalities and had a deep understanding of the regional differences, loyalties and religious mindset of the people. The Redemptorists accepted the challenge and sent Father Joseph MUELLER, C.Ss.R., to become the 6th pastor of St. Michaels. His message at his first mass on Sunday, February 26, 1860 was one of unity and appealing to his parishioners spiritual needs. A hopeful start, Mueller won over several parish families immediately with his conciliatory tone. Yes, it took the dedication of the Redemptorists and the charismatic pastor taken from their ranks to build a parish to last for one hundred and fifty-six years!

Aha, gentle reader, you ask for more on the Redemptorists? This brief history should help answer your questions. The Redemptorists order, officially known as the Congregation of the Most Holy Redeemer, trace their roots back to 1732 when they were formed by St. Alphonsus Liguori in Italy (in those days the territory was part of the Kingdom of Naples). Their original mission was to care for the overlooked and forgotten country peasants and farmers around Naples.

The group, popular from the very start because of their saintly and charismatic founder, soon spread from the shadow of Mount Vesuvius throughout the Italian peninsula.

The Redemptorists adopted the simple vows of poverty, chastity and obedience. They follow a rule "to strive to imitate the virtues and examples of Jesus Christ, Our Redeemer, consecrating themselves especially to the preaching of the word of God to the poor."

Redemptorists staff many Catholic parishes and are known as outstanding mission preachers, retreat masters and parish missionaries.

In the late 1700s, Redemptorists began ministries and houses in German-speaking regions as well as in Poland. Although the Redemptorists were often swept up into the exacerbating political movements of the times, their influence continued to spread, moving into Switzerland, Austria, Belgium and Holland in the 1800s. Politics often interfered with Redemptorist ministries and the order was regularly banished from locales only to be reinstated when the climate changed.

Redemptorists first arrived in North America in 1832 as three Austrian members of the order came to minister to German populations as well as Indians in Michigan and Ohio. Their expertise in dealing with the difficulties of the disputes of Catholic Germans from many different backgrounds first was celebrated in Pittsburgh, where they calmed and transformed a bitterly embattled German parish into a model of cooperation and devotion.

Reputation solidly in hand, the Redemptorists became the prevalent order ministering to German Catholic immigrants in many U.S. cities and dioceses. An American Province was founded in 1850, eventually divided in 1875, with Provincial administrations in St. Louis and Baltimore.

The Redemptorist skill at knowing and dealing with the special pressures and circumstances of the German immigrant community and German Catholics made them the logical choice, when in 1860, Rt. Rev. James J. Duggan, 4th Bishop of Chicago, called upon them to help solve the disputes and problems raging in the 8-year-old St. Michael's Parish in Chicago's Old Town neighborhood.

The members of the Congregation of the Most Holy Redeemer have staffed and brought visionary leadership to the parish for 150 years.

Hmmm, let us begin to conclude this Reverie by including a synopsis of Roman Catholicism in Germany today. With about 28.2 million members, the Roman Catholic church in unified Germany is organized into five archdioceses, eighteen dioceses, three diocesan offices, and one apostolic administration. Two of the archdioceses are based in Bavaria (Munich/Freising and Bamberg) and two in North Rhine-Westphalia (Cologne and Paderborn). More than 57 percent of all German Roman Catholics live in these two Lander. Another 28 percent live in the three Lander of Baden-Wurttemberg, Hesse, and Rhineland-Palatinate. Only about 900 of the church's 13,000 parishes and other pastoral centers are located in the new Lander. The number of Roman Catholics in East Germany declined from 2 million shortly after the war to 800,000 by 1992. Serving these Roman Catholics are two dioceses, one in Brandenburg (Berlin) and the other in Saxony (Dresden).

Between 1970 and 1989, the number of Roman Catholics attending Sunday mass in West Germany declined from 37 percent to 23 percent. Between 1970 and 1990, the number of annual baptisms fell from about 370,000 to around 300,000. Approximately 470,000 Roman Catholics officially left the church between 1985 and 1990. In the same period, about 25,000 returned to the church, and another 25,000 converted to other religions.

Despite the diminishing numbers of Roman Catholics, the church tax enables the Roman Catholic Church to remain strong financially. In 1992 the church's share of tax revenues amounted to approximately DM8.5 billion. An additional DM8 billion was received in the form of government subsidies, service payments, property, and contributions. Much of this support is returned to society through an extensive network of church-operated kindergartens, senior citizen centers, and hospitals. The main Roman Catholic charitable organization is the Deutscher Caritasverband, which had about 400,000 employees in 1992.

As the FRG has become an increasingly secular society, the centuries-old traditional authority of the Roman Catholic Church in matters of morality has declined, especially among German youth. Man German Roman Catholics routinely ignore the church and in particular the pope's positions on such key issues as birth control, premarital sex, divorce, and abortion. For years the number of ordinations in Germany has declined. To address this issue, most German Catholics favor permitting priests to marry, and many support the ordination of women.

Peridically, independent reformist clergymen challenge the church hierarchy and doctrine. Often they do so with the support of many German Catholics. In the 1870s, Hans Kung, a theologian at Tubingen University, used his position and charisma to criticize the idea of papal infallibility and other dogmas. In the early 1990s, major differences of opinion between the laity and church authorities were revealed by a clash between a reform-minded priest and the archbishop in Paderborn, the most conservative German diocese. For beliefs deemed contrary to Vatican policies and dogma, Father Eugen Drewermann was defrocked by Archbishop Johannes Degenhardt. In the tradition of Luther, Drewermann continued to express his unorthodox views outside the church—at universities and in the media, including talk shows. A 1992 survey indicated that among all Germans, Drewermann was more popular than Pope John Paul II.

Before ending the reverie, we must mention some of German's contributions to the happiness of the world. In the world of music: the three "Bs" of classical music (1.) Johann Sebastian Bach, 1685-1750, organist and composer, (2.) Ludwig Van Beethoven, 1770-1827, composer, (3.) Johannes Brahms, 1833-1897, composer and pianist. Now, if we add to them the operas of Wilhelm Richard Wagner, 1813-1883, poet and composer, especially "Die Meistersinger" and "The Ring Cycle," plus the magnificent compositions and choral arrangements of the German born composer George Frederic Handel, 1685-1750, especially his "Messiah," plus every 10 years, the Village of Oberammergau presents the outside performance of the Passion Play of Jesus Christ and invites the whole world to come and see. Yes and this is only a small list of the many Germans that have made the lives of the people of the world more enjoyable and happier and better. Also, the name we have read so many times in history must be mentioned for our own reflection, the name of Prince Otto Edward Leopold Bismarck, 1815-1898, the first Chancellor of the German Empire.

Let us finally end this reverie with a short account of and a prayer to two very famous German saints.

(1.) St. Henry (972-1024) descended on both sides from Charlemagne, he was the son of Henry, Duke of Bavaria, and Gisela of Burgundy. He succeeded his father as duke (995), became king of Germany (1002) and Holy Roman Emperor (1014). He married St. Cunegundo (998) but had no children. His study with St. Wolfgang of Regensburg kindled a lifelong interest in ecclesiastical affairs that merged with his secular power. He created the See of Bamberg (1006), built its cathedral, and supported the reform initiated by the monks of Cluny in France. He was renowned as a just ruler, a man of prayer, and a humble ascetic. Like him, may we find ways to unify our religious and everyday lives.

(2.) St. Boniface, bishop and martyr (675-754), was born in England. Wynfrid was raised in Benedictine monasteries. A renowned teacher and preacher, he went as a missionary to Friesland (northern Netherlands), where he worked with Saint Willibrord (716). Pope Gregory II gave him the name Boniface, along with a commission to preach to non-Christians (719). He was made bishop of Germany (722). At Geismar, Boniface made numerous conversions when he cut down the sacred pagan Oak of Thor without being harmed by their gods. On June 5, 754, he and 30 companions were killed by non-Christians while preparing to confirm more converts. His work as missionary, organizer and reformer earned him the title of "Apostle of Germany." Like Boniface, let us pray to "stand fast in what is right, and prepare our souls for trial." St. Boniface wrote "In her voyage across the ocean of this world, the Church is like a great ship being pounded by the waves of life's different stresses. Our duty is not to abandon ship but to keep her on her course."

We can not meditate in October especially here at RRC without thinking about Our Lady of the Rosary (October 7). In ancient times, Marian feasts of the Eastern Church centered on events in Mary's life. Since the 12th century, Marian celebrations in the Western calendar usually recall a particular event of the times. Today's memorial began in the late 15th century by some confraternities of the Rosary, and in 1571 was solemnized by Pius V in thanksgiving for the victory of the Christian navy over the Turks at the battle of Lepanto near Corinth. In 1716, Clement XI extended the memorial to the universal church. May we discover how praying the rosary "nourishes our faith, which flourishes again by meditation on the sacred mysteries, and raises minds to the truth revealed to us by God" (PiusXI).

GOTT SEGNE DEICH
(GOD BLESS YOU)

I will give you the kingdom that my Father gave to Me, and in that kingdom you will eat and drink at My table. (Luke 22:29-30)

AUF WEIDERSEHN
(I'll see you again)

Bert Hoffman

Addendum One: Germany-A Reverie October, 2007

This article was written about St. Michael Church, 455 West Eugenie Street (1700 North) by my good friend, George A. Lane, S.J. in his book "Chicago Churches and Synagogues", published by Loyola University Press in 1981.

Historic St. Michael's has been called "Chicago's best kept secret." The parish was founded in 1852 as more and more German immigrants came to Chicago and settled north of the river in an area known until the 1940s as North Town. Land for the new church was donated by Michael Diversey of the Diversey and Lill Brewery and the church was named for his patron saint. Diversey Avenue also commemorates this early Chicago brewer.

The Redemptorist fathers took charge of St. Michael's in 1860 and the cornerstone for the new church was laid in 1866. Constructed of red brick with elaborate limestone trim in a Romanesque style, St. Michael's was 190 feet long and 80 feet wide, cost $131,000, and was completed and dedicated in 1869.

The Great Fire of 1871 destroyed the whole North Town neighborhood and gutted St. Michael's leaving only the walls of the church and part of the tower standing. The Daily Tribune reported St. Michael's to be "the most imposing ruins on the north side." But the industrious parishioners soon rebuilt the church and it was rededicated on October 12, 1873.

The five great bells, weighing between 2,500 and 6,000 pounds each, named for St. Michael, St. Mary, St. Joseph, St. Alphonsus, and St. Theresa, were blessed and installed in 1876. Local tradition has it that anyone who can hear the bells of St. Michael's is a resident of Old Town.

The tower of St. Michael's with its illuminated four-sided clock is a landmark on the Near North Side. It rises 290 feet above Old Town, was completed in 1888, and is visible for miles around. The cross on the top of the steeple is 24 by 9 feet and weighs 2,235 pounds. The main façade of this church is on Eugenie Street. Its gabled, three-portal main entrance recalls the cathedrals of Europe and like them represents the three persons of the Blessed Trinity. The tripartite theme is carried through on the façade by the three large window openings above and behind the main entrance. A nine-foot statue of St. Michael, sent to the parish in 1913 by a Bavarian stonecutter, is located above the central arch and is flanked by Corinthian columns. Brick corbelling with limestone trim beneath and limestone eaves above completes the main portion of this north elevation.

The interior of St. Michael's has been redecorated many times, but always with the off-white, gold, and light blue motif characteristic of Bavarian baroque church interiors. Five altars, including the permanent altar with its 56 foot high reredos (an ornamental screen or wall of wood or stone located behind an altar), were built and installed by Hacker and Son of La Crosse, Wisconsin in 1902. High above the permanent altar a statue of St. Michael stands in conquest over the fallen angels.

The altar on the west side of the church in honor of Mary, Mother of Perpetual Help, enshrines a painting that was entrusted to the Redemptorist fathers by pope Pius IX in 1865. This picture is said to have miraculously survived the Fire of 1871 and it is especially dear to the parishioners.

The exceptionally tall stained glass windows of St. Michael's were supplied by Mayer & Company of Munich in 1902.

The three-manual Kilgen organ with 37 ranks and 2,236 pipes was installed in 1925.

St. Michael's Church is still the center and its tower the identifying mark of the Old Town neighborhood which has enjoyed a revitalization that began in the 1930s and continues to this day.

Addendum Two: Germany-A Reverie October 2007

This article was submitted by my good friend Anna Hubert who is also a resident at R.R.C. for the October issue of Phoenix, a monthly publication of the Resurrection Retirement Community.

The Federal Republic of Germany is situated in the heart of Europe and has the largest population in the European Union: About 82 million people live there. Germany shares its borders with nine neighboring countries: Denmark to the north, the Netherlands, Belgium, Luxembourg and France to the west, Switzerland and Austria to the south, and the Czech Republic and Poland to the east.

For many years following World War II, there were two German states. Germany was defeated in 1945 by the United States, Britain, France and the Soviet Union. Not long thereafter, the Cold War led to the division of Germany into an eastern part, the German Democratic Republic (GDR, also called East Germany), and a western part, the Federal Republic of Germany; a border divided the two sections. The city of Berlin was also split: in 1961 the East German government put a wall right through the middle of the city.

The GDR was a product of the Soviet Union and was built on the foundations of a dictatorial system enforced by the Soviet army. Under this strict system, people made several attempts to gain more freedom. But it was not until 1989 that the mass demonstrations triggered the fall of the Berlin Wall. In the autumn of that year, tens of thousands of East German citizens fled to the West through other countries. On November 9, 1989, the Berlin Wall was opened; one year later, East Germany joined West Germany to become one country.

October 3, 1990 was the day of German unification and that date is now celebrated each year as a national holiday. The German people, government and economy were faced with enormous challenges when the integration of the two very different political, economic and educational systems began. Since then much has been achieved though more challenges lie ahead. While the country was divided, the Federal Republic's seat of government was provisionally in Bonn, a small city on the Rhine River. The German Democratic Republic was governed from East Berlin. In 1990, the capital was restored to Berlin, a geographic symbol of unification.

Today, Germany is a democratic republic. It has a house of representatives, called the Bundestag, and a second chamber, called the Bundesrat, which represents Germany's 16 federal states. Unlike the U.S., however, the Federal Republic has both a president, who acts as head of state, and a chancellor, who runs the federal government.

HISTORY

The ancient Romans used the name "Germany" for all the tribes that spoke Germanic languages or dialects. This is where the English word "German" comes from. Deutsch, which is what the Germans call themselves, comes from the root "theodisk," which meant "the people." When the Romans ruled the western world, they build fortress towns for their military. From their period of domination in what is now Germany, remnants of Roman architecture remain, especially in cities like Augsburg, Regensburg, Trier and Cologne.

In the Middle Ages, Germany was a patchwork of small states ruled by kings, princes and dukes. These rulers built castles that can still be found all over Germany, especially along the Rhine and Saale rivers. The common people lived in villages that were built outside the castle walls; as in other European countries, the majority were poor peasants who did not own land and had no rights. Over the centuries more and more towns were built up and these became flourishing cities. Their citizens were merchants, crafts people artisans and trade people. Many peasants moved to the towns, too, because they were granted rights there. This movement still lives on in German proverbs such as "Stadtluft macht frei" (urban air frees you).

The 19th century brought industrialization and unification to the German states. In 1871, Otto von Bismarck unified Germany for the first time. The imperialism of Germany and the other European powers led to the outbreak of World War I in August 1914. At the western front in France, battles soon turned into trench warfare, with enormous losses on both sides. The United States' entry into the war in 1917 brought the final military defeat of Germany and its ally Austria.

GERMANY

World War I brought many political changes in Europe. For Germany it meant becoming a republic, (the so called Weimar Republic of 1919-1932).

Suffering from the great depression, the harsh peace conditions dictated by the Treaty of Versailles and a long succession of more or less unstable government caused anger among the public which suffered from high unemployment and poverty. During this trying time the anti democratic, anti semitic National Socialist movement of Adolf Hitler became a leading force and by 1932 the largest single Party in Germany.

President Paul von Hindenburg seeing little alternative and pushed by right wing advisers appointed Adolf Hitler Chancellor of Germany on January 30, 1933. In 1939 the growing tensions from nationalism, militarism and territorial issues leading the Germans to launching the Blitzkrieg on September 1 against Poland and World War II.

Curious to learn more facts about Germany? Visit our website at: *www.germany-info.org* or, write to the consulate of the Federal Republic of Germany nearest to you. For more information about the consulates, also see the website above.

Submitted by: Anna Hubert

ADDENDUM THREE: GERMANY-A REVERIE
October 2007

At Your Side There Were Germans Too
By Konrad Krez
(Published in October 2007 Phoenix)

Not as burdens to these shores we throng, from
our cherished German fatherland.
Indeed, we have brought so much along, unknown to you, yet by our hand.
And when from the dense forestall shields, and the open
wilderness you wreath'd your vast and verdant fields,
at your side there were Germans too.

So much of that which in earlier days you brought here from across the sea,
we taught you how to prepare, and ways to produce more goods, yes, 'twas we.
Dare not forget this, deny it n'er-
Say not that we did not so do,
For a thousand forges witness bear:
At your side there were Germans too.
And though your art and your sciences now bring their strength
and power to this land, their fame rests still on the German brow,
'twas mostly done by German hand, and when from your songs
melodies ring memories of hearts once so true, 'tis known to me,
in the songs you sing is much put there by Germans too!
Thus, with great pride on this soil we stand, which from the
wilds our strength brought claim, ever wonder then, what
kind of land, 'twould be if n'er a German came!
And so we declared in Lincoln's day, and that day freedom's horn first
blew-yes, we dare undeniably say: At your side there were Germans too!

BACKGROUND OF THE SCROLL

Konrad Krez emigrated to the U.S.A. from Germany in 1850 and soon became a successful district attorney and lawyer. During the Civil War he rose to the rank of Brigadoon General in the Union Army. Considered the greatest German-American poet of the 19th century, General Krez composed hundreds of poems, among which are to be found the famous lyrics inscribed on this scroll:

"Da waren Deutsche auch dabei."
"At your side there were Germans too."

ADDENDUM FOUR: GERMANY—A REVERIE
October 2007

A group of us left Resurrection Retirement Community to tour St. Michael's on October 11, 2007. We were met at the church doors by a welcoming committee, each of which highlighted some notable and famous historic point of interest. We were each given the following pamphlet entitled "Historic St. Michael's Church in Old Town.

OLD ST. MICHAEL'S
Called "one of Chicago's best kept secrets", the church that survived the Great Fire displays its proud past in this the centennial year.
Written by James Reddy (in1952)

The great bells in St. Michael's tower began to toll, slowly, sonorously. It was mid-morning, October 9, a bright, dry day, a little more than two years since Bishop Luers had come all the way from Fort Wayne to dedicate the imposing new church. St. Michael's was old even then; a church whose history went back to 1848 when Michael Diversey donated the land. His family name is perpetuated in Diversey Boulevard, his Christian name in the church dedicated to his patron, Saint Michael. Now as the fire moved northward, it was threatened.

People hoped the fire could be stopped at the Chicago River. But gusts of wind blew flaming debris across the water to the grain elevators on the northern bank. In the early morning of October 9 the fire began to devour the North Side. The wooden roof of the pumping station went up in a blaze, leaving the city without water, and the gas works exploded with a roar.

Called by the tolling of the bells, the German parishioners filled the wood-cobbled streets and planked sidewalks, hoping the massive walls of St. Michael's would resist the fire. When the crowd saw the Alexian Brothers Hospital go up in flames, they knew their parish would burn. Pastor Peter Zimmer and a group of priests and helpers dashed about the church, scooping up what they could, hurrying to the Monastery garden to bury the salvaged treasure. The large wooden crucifix that hung in the convent's lower corridor was dismantled and buried along with other treasures and many volumes from the library. Father Charles Hahn returned from a northern suburb with a team and wagon, which they loaded with vestments, the hand-carved stations of the cross, and as much clothing as they could gather. Then the sisters clambered aboard and they set out for safety at Rosehill.

Clapboard houses on all sides of the church wrinkled and withered in fire. Some called it an ocean of flames, describing it as a breaker a mile long, leaping like waves 300-feet into the air, blowing smoke, sparks and lighted shingles in every direction. Over the roar of the fire, shouts and the tolling of the bells, explosions were heard as the fire force blew up buildings.

They watched as the church took fire. Finally great shafts of flame and burning debris smashed the east side window and entered the church.

Alight like a torch held aloft in the darkened sky, the upper section of the bell tower burned and began to crumble. The huge bells hurtled from their tower with a dull thud and melted into a toneless mass of bronze. The fire passed on.

By nine-o'clock on the evening of the ninth, the fire had gotten as far as the city's outskirts at Fullerton Avenue. Beyond Fullerton the fire didn't have much to feed on. Rain began to fall. Pastor Zimmer, the clergy staff and a handful of parishioners returned on Tuesday morning to survey the debris through a pall of smoke and smoldering embers. Gone were the priests' home, the sisters' convent, the school. But miraculously, St. Michael's stood. The solid brick and stone walls, the soaring Corinthian columns had survived the fire; stood then as they would stand when the church was restored.

The burning of their church fired the determination of St. Michael's parishioners. They set about propping up the now freestanding columns, began clearing the rubble away. They shoveled piles of ashes and debris into the catacomb of tunnels that ran beneath the old church. Today, one hundred years later, visitors to St. Michael's can see the ashes of the Great Fire of 1871. (While the ashes are still in the basement of the church, they are no longer accessible.)

After much of the charred mass was cleared away, they came upon the picture of Our Mother of Perpetual Help. It had withstood the fire and intense heat without damage. But the wooden crucifix, books and (many) other treasures buried in the monastery garden were gone. The parishioners wasted very little time on self pity, and with typical German industry, set about rebuilding their homes and church. Soon temporary wooden huts dotted the neighborhood around St. Michael's. Temporarily the fathers stayed in Rosehill. On Sunday, October 15, Pastor Zimmer said Mass for the people in a private home. During the week, Brothers Adam, Theobold, and Adrian, with the help of a local carpenter, put up a ninety foot wooden shanty. Its back wall was stone for the shanty was propped against the old garden wall. One end of this structure served as shelter for an open-air altar. On Sunday, October 22, the first two services were offered in this shelter.

In early November a temporary building was erected on Hurlburt (Cleveland Avenue). The lower floors provided space for the school, and later when the church was completely restored, the entire building was used as a school. Two years earlier the church had cost $131.251, and now with the donated labor of the priests and parish, damage to the structure was repaired at a cost of $40,000 (plus insurance). The church was rededicated about a year later on October 12, 1872.

It was not until 1876, however, that the bells returned. According to the church records they were cast in bronze by the McShane Co., and named after St. Michael, St. Mary, St. Joseph, St. Alphonsus and St. Theresa. These are the melodious bells that Oldtowners hear today as they sound the quarter, half and hour. With a low bow in the direction of St. Mary-le-Bow, whose bells are said to sound throughout Cockney England, they say you live in Old Town if you can hear the bells in St. Michael's tower.

That same year of 1876 saw the completion of the parish house, and the installation of tinted glass to replace the temporary translucent windows. But it was September 16, 1902, that the sixteen leaded and stained glass windows created by the Mayer Window Art Institute of Munich, Germany, were installed. These windows are ranked high among the beautiful examples of German ecclesiastic art glass still to be seen in this country.

The great day to St. Michael's history came on October 12, 1873, when the parishioners celebrated the resurrection of their church. Marching bands from St. Joseph's, St. Boniface, St. Anthony's and other parishes awakened the slumbering city with exuberant Teutonic marches. The bands met at Erie Street and began a two mile long triumphant parade to the doors of St. Michael's. They drew up before a huge wreath on the corner of Hurlburt and Linden, (Cleveland and Eugenie) inscribed in grand gold letters, with the cheery, if slightly prosaic message:

"Welcome you, friends, from far and near,
To bless this, the house of the Lord most dear."

St. Michael's doors are still open to bless or entertain you and welcomes all to help celebrate its resurrection in this centennial year (of 1952).

ADDENDUM FIVE: GERMANY—A REVERIE
October 2007

I certainly must mention my namesake St. Albert the Great, Bishop and Doctor of the Church (c.1200-1280). Born in Germany, he studied at the University of Padua where he joined the Dominicans (1229). After teaching in Germany, he went to the University of Paris (1240-44) and taught theology there (1245-48). Thomas Aquinas was his student. He returned to Cologne to teach the Dominicans. Despite his protests, the Pope appointed him Bishop of Ratisbon (1260) but four years later he resigned to return to teaching. Called "The Great" (Magnus) for his intellectual gifts, he was a philosopher, natural scientist, theologian, administrator and teacher, and a keen student of Arabic learning and culture. He was the chief pioneer in adapting Aristotle's philosophy for thology. Declared a doctor of the church (1931), he is a patron saint of scientists. May we follow his advice that "it is by the path of love, which is charity, that God draws near to us, and we to God." His feast day is November 15. "Knowledge of Divine things is imprinted on our minds by union with God, just as the wax molds itself into the seal—not the reverse." St. Albert the Great.

Wisdom 7:22-8: l.) In Wisdom is a spirit intelligent, holy, unique, manifold, subtle, agile, clear, unstained, certain, not baneful, loving the good, keen, unhampered, beneficent, kindly, firm, secure, tranquil, all powerful, all seeing, and pervading all spirits, though they be intelligent, pure and very subtle. For wisdom is mobile beyond all motion, and she penetrates and pervades all things by reason of her purity. For she is an aura of the might of God and a pure effusion of the glory of the Almighty; Therefore nought that is sullied enters into her. For she is the refulgence of eternal light, the spotless mirror of the power of God, the image of His goodness. And passing into holy souls from age to age, she produces friends of God and prophets.

Holy Mary, Seat of Wisdom, Pray For Us!!

INDIA—A REVERIE

To softly introduce our reverie on India, let us go back thousands of years in time to the land in Asia between the Arabian Sea and the Bay of Bengal. There are many, many rivers in this area but the one river that tribes and groups of people found very accommodating to settlements was the GANGES. This river was about 1667 miles long found today in N and NE India and flows south and the southeast from the Himalayas to merge with the Brahmaputra River and then flows into the Bay of Bengal through the Ganges delta.

As the centuries passed by more and more settlements were established along the Ganges River. Eventually, many settlements produced seers and sages, men who were eminent in wisdom, prudence, very sensible, and exercised good judgment. These men wrote about a way of life and eventually these writing were put in books. The Ganges became a sacred river. This was the beginning of Hinduism.

Hinduism today commands the adherence of approximately 850 million people in the world. Thus every 7th human being is a Hindu. This makes Hinduism the third largest religion in the world after Christianity (approx. 2 billion) and Islam (1.3 billion). These figures certainly give the impression that Hinduism is a world religion. However, a look at the geographical spread of Hindus reveal that this impression is deceptive. From the Encyclopedia Britannica, we read that the number of Hindus in millions in India are 800, in Nepal are 20, in Bangladesh are 16, in Pakistan are 2, for a total of 838 million. These countries border on India. It is clear that more than 95% of all Hindus reside in India and approximately 98% in South Asia. The two predominant reasons for the geographical confinement of Hinduism are: 1.) traditionally, Hinduism is a non-proselytizing religion, i.e., Hindus do not normally convert people of other faiths to their own. This contrasts totally with the record of Semitic faiths like Christianity and Islam.

2.) In the last few centuries, Hindus in many countries have suffered severe reverses due to absorption by or conversion to other religions or massacres and persecution leading to migrations to India or conversion to other faiths.

For Hinduism there is not revelation of God or of the absolute. Hindu scripture, based on the insights of Hindu sages and seers, serves primarily as a guidebook. But ultimately truth comes through direct consciousness of the divine or the ultimate reality. In other religions this ultimate reality is known as God. Hindus refer to it by many names, but the most common name is Brahman. What follows now are eleven paragraphs concerning commonly asked questions about Hinduism.

Hinduism is not a religion in the strict sense of the word. It is recommendation for living a disciplined, pure and blissful life needed for God realization. The word religion comes from the Latin "religio" which means binding the soul back to God. Other religions have strict laws and beliefs to attain this God realization. Hindus, however, do not believe in such strict laws. The desire to free one's self from worldly bondage and to obtain a better present and next life through proper karma (actions) in the present life is the basis of the Hindu way of life. Your karma (good or bad actions) returns to you with results and acts as your teacher to guide you in the right directions in the life. The guidelines for better living to achieve such a liberation (modsha) was revealed directly by God to our ancient sages who used to meditate constantly for the welfare of all human beings. These revelations are the contents of the Vedas, our fundamental scripture. It is also called sanatana dharma, an eternal discipline of life or Vedic dharma, the proper way of living based on Vedas. Hindus believe that every human being is divine by nature and the purpose of life is to expose that divinity to the fullest possible extent. Based on the Vedic recommendations, Hindus believe in one formless and all pervading God called Brahma who is the creator of the universe and represents the supreme truth.

For all practical purposes, in the modern times the Hindu way of life is called Hinduism. It is the oldest living religion on earth. Because of its basic philosophies the Hindu religion can be considered a universal religion.

The main difference between Hinduism and other religions is that Hinduism did not evolve out of the teachings of any one saint, prophet or messiah. Instead, the vedic thoughts were obtained by various sages over the centuries. A very big difference is the Hinduism teaches reincarnation, or rebirth of soul. Moreover, Hinduism is a very accommodating and compassionate religion. Coexistence with other religions with respect and humbleness is the core of the Hindu way of life. Hindus not only love their neighbors but they also love and pray for everyone. A Hindu life is meant for humanity and is achieved through uplifting of one's morality.

The Vedas are the original scriptures of Hinduism on which the entire Hindu way of life is based. The ethical way of living as suggested in the Vedas is called dharma. Dharma is God's divine law for discipline and proper development of human beings. By Vedas no particular book is meant. The revelations that the ancient seekers of truth received through meditations were transferred from generation to generation through oral teachings. Many of those spoken concepts have been compiled and are available in volumes that we now call the Vedas. The Vedas are a collection of hymns, prayers, rituals, benedictions, sacrificial formulas and chants. There are four distinct Vedas: Rig Veda, Yajur Veda, Sam Veda and Atharva Veda. Rig Veda the oldest among the Vedas mainly consists of hymns and chants praising God; Yajur Veda contains divine verses in musical form; and Atharva Veda contains guidelines for the proper way of living. The four Vedas were revealed to the sages Agni, Vayu, Aditaya and Angira respectively. Later the Vedas were systemized for human benefit by sage Vyas.

Each of the Vedas contains similar essential details on how to lead a life with a sound body, mind, and intellect and also how to attain a better next life. Each Veda consists of a ritual part and a philosophical part. The philosophical part of Vedas is called Upanishad. There are 108 Upanishads in all.

The word reincarnation literally means coming again into physical body. According to our scriptures, a soul passes into a body at birth and migrates into another body at death. The change of the bodies is just like putting a new garment and discarding it when it is worn out. The kind of body the soul enters into at death is determined by one's actions (karma) in present life. A person's karma determines in what form he will reappear. He may come back in a higher (human) or lower (animal) life form. Good karma in the present life leads to a better next life and bad karma in the present life leads to a worst next life. This cycle of rebirth continues until one achieves liberation from worldly bondage (moksha). At the liberated stage a soul becomes godly and reincarnation stops.

"Om" is the most sacred syllable often spoken during the practice of any Hindu rites. It is a holy character (letter) of the Sanskrit language, the language of God. The character is a composite of three different letters of the Sanskrit alphabet. The English equivalent of those are "a", "u", and "m", and represent the Hindu Trinity. The Trinity is composed of the three supreme Hindu Gods: Brahma, the creator, Vishnu, the preserver, and Shiva, the destroyer. These three letters when pronounced properly in unison create an invigorating effect in the body. Because of its significance this sacred syllable is spoken before any chants to show God we remember Him. Another very important sign is Swastika which is regarded as divine by Hindus. The word swastika means 'auspicious' in the Sanskrit language and hence is used to symbolize the welcoming of auspiciousness and driving away evils. The symbol also represents the changing of the universe around the unchanging nature of God. The symbol is a mirror image of the one that was abused by groups such as the Nazis during World War II. Om is not similar to amen. Amen is spoken to assert faith at the end of a religious proclamation and Om is spoken to invoke the presence of God before any religious recitation.

Actually, Hindus believe in only one formless and all-pervading, all-existing, and all-blissful God. That formless God, however, can best be realized by concentrating on various forms of ideal personalities as recorded in the scriptures. In other words, the Hindu religion is flexible and provides many ways to develop one's spiritual ideas in order to suit individual needs. "Unity in the diverse plan of nature" is recognized in the Hindu faith. Just as people tailor clothes to fit their needs, Hindus have different gods and goddesses for their religious needs. All these gods and goddesses resemble humans, animals or natural forces such as wind, water, fire, sun, and moon; each has different powers to bless the world. These godheads, when worshipped, fulfill people's desires in an easier way but with the same qualities of blessings as from one God.

The caste system was an important part of the Hindu way of life. During the Vedic age a social classification system called Varnashrama was devised so that the human race could have a smooth and ordered life in society. The system created the castes of Brahmins, the intellectual class, Kshatriyas, the warrior class, Vaishyas, the trader class and Shudras, the service people. Don't you see that every society has a need for teachers and/or preachers, defense, trade and commerce, and service even today? Our forefathers realized this need for order in society even then. Of course, the original concept of social order has been abused over the ages into its present mutilated form. The original caste system also supported the moving of individuals from one caste to another based on one's actions and performance in society. Isn't this concept of Hinduism true in modern living? Of course, it is.

Hindus seek enlightenment through Yoga. Yoga is a vast system of seeking spirituality in life by controlling body and mind. The word itself means "union with God." There are several paths for achieving this union and there are several Yogas mentioned in our scriptures. One of many Yogas is Hatha Yoga and deals with physical exercises for good health. Asanas and breath control system is called pranayama. These asanas and pranayamas are based on activating the seven coiled energy centers in the human body called chakras. It is logical that good health will induce a sound mind, hence better concentration on God can be realized. It is this particular Yoga, which is only a small part of the Hindu Yoga system that you often hear about in the western world.

Our scriptures show us ways to obtain a sound body and mind in order to lead a proper way of life. Proper intake of food is necessary for this purpose. Hence the scriptures recommend only those foods which are tasty and can be digested easily and such foods are said to be in the "mode of goodness" (satwik). Vegetarian food by nature falls in this category. Although our scriptures do not say specifically not to eat non-vegetarian food, but they do emphasize the mode of goodness considerations in selecting the foods we eat. The selection between the two types of foods is up to the individual, though, of course, most Hindus choose to eat vegetarian food only. Let's end these paragraphs by repeating the main Hindu gods: Shiva, often seen as the destroyer of the world; Visnu, often seen as the preserver of the world's order; Brahma, often seen as the creator; Dayvi, the goddess.

Well, gentle reader, let's now read about the introduction of Christianity into India in the first century by introducing one of the twelve apostles; namely, St. Thomas. From a few verses in the Gospel of John, St. Thomas the apostle emerges as one of the most vivid characters in the New Testament. When Jesus announces his desire to proceed toward Jerusalem, it is Thomas who issues the bold challenge, "Let us also go, that we may die with him" (11:16). Later, at the Last Supper, when Jesus speaks in a cryptic fashion about the way he is going, Thomas asks, "Lord, we do not know where you are going; how can we know the way?" This evokes the famous response: "I am the way, and the truth, and the life; no one comes to the Father, but by me" (14:5).

But it is for his famous "doubt" that Thomas is chiefly remembered. After Easter, Thomas reacts incredulously to the report of his fellow apostles that they have seen the Risen Lord. He will never believe, he insists, unless he can feel for himself the marks of the nails and place his hand in Christ's wounded side.

Eight days later Christ appears to all of them in the "upper room" where they are hiding. Addressing Thomas by name he invites the doubting disciple to touch his wounds, to place his hand in his side. To this invitation Thomas simply exclaims, "My Lord and my God!" So Jesus responds, "Have you believed because you have seen me? Blessed are those who have not seen and yet believe" (20:24-30).

At the St. Thomas Day celebration in New Delhi on December 18, 1955, Dr. Rajendra Prasad, the then President of India, said: "St. Thomas came to India when many of the countries of Europe had not yet become Christian, and so those Indians who trace their Christianity to him have a longer history and a higher ancestry than that of Christians of many of the European countries."

It would be appropriate to cite here an extract from the radio message of Pope Pius XII on 31 December, 1952 on the occasion of the 19th century celebrations of the arrival of the Apostle in India: "Nineteen hundred years have passed since the Apostle came to India. During the centuries that India was cut off from the West and despite many trying vicissitudes, the Christian communities formed by the Apostle conserved intact the legacy he left them. This apostolic lineage, beloved sons and daughters, is the proud privilege of the many among you who glory in the name of Thomas Christians and we are happy on this occasion to acknowledge and bear witness to it."

There are people who doubt about the apostolate of St. Thomas in India. However, according to the tradition, St. Thomas, one of the twelve apostles of Jesus Christ, came to India in 52 A.D., and landed at Kodungallur on the Malabar (presently Kerala) coast. He preached the Gospel to the Brahmin families of Kerala, many of whom received the faith. He established seven Churches there. It is also a tradition that he frequently visited Malayattoor hills for prayer. Later, he moved on to the east coast of India. He was martyred in 72 A.D. by a fanatic at Little Mount (near Madras) and his body was brought to Mylapore (near Madras) and was buried there. His tomb is venerated until this day.

This tradition is confirmed by the testimonies of many of the Fathers of the church. It was not difficult for the Apostle to come to India, because extensive trade relations existed between Malabar and the Mediterranean countries even before the Christian era. There is nothing to contradict this tradition.

Here is an additional comment to ponder: Thomas shares the lot of Peter the Impetuous, James and John, the "Sons of Thunder," Philip and his foolish request to see the Father; indeed all the apostles in their weakness and lack of understanding. We must not exaggerate these facts, however, for Christ did not pick worthless men. But their human weakness again points up the fact that holiness is a gift of God, not a human creation; it is given to ordinary men and women with weaknesses, it is God who gradually transforms the weaknesses into the image of Christ, the courageous, trusting and loving one.

Since India is the last nation included in our International Year it might be beneficial to include some missionary activities in Asia and Africa since they are the fastest growing Catholic continents. So, to do this, let us leap ahead in time and turn our attention to the missions in the Seventeenth Century. But first, Christopher Columbus found America accidentally when he sailed in the year 1491 to find out a sea-route to kerala, the land of spices. In Kerala varieties of spice grow abundantly. The western world bought the spices from Kerala, that gave flavor to the foods of the west. Kerala is one of 25 states comprising the Indian Union, which is the largest Democratic Republic in the world. This is the southernmost state which is on the shores of the Arabian Sea. There is no unanimous opinion among the scholars as regards to the origin of the name "Kerala." Suffice it to say, the name more often used by European writers for "Kerala" is "Malabar." Extensive trade relations existed between Malabar and the Mediterranean countries even before the Christian Era. The peculiar geography, with a range of mountains, separated Kerala from the rest of India, but opened it to the foreigner through sea. People from far and wide, came in search of the "Black Gold" (pepper) and other spices. It is a land of great beauty with hills, rivers, forests and backwaters making it a rare spectacle. Now back to the missions.

The missionary activity begun in the 1500's took on new life in the 1600s. In 1622, Pope Gregory XV founded the congregation for the Propagation of the Faith. The Vatican office coordinated the efforts of all missionary groups. In 1627 the College of Urban was set up in Rome to train missionaries. The Vatican also created a new position called the vicar-apostolic; a vicar-apostolic had the authority of a bishop, was responsible to Rome, but was not tied to one specific territory.

One such vicar-apostolic, Matthew de Castro, a convert from Hinduism, went back home to India after training in Rome. He educated Indian clergy and handed over his work to two Indian successors. By the mid-1700s the church was well established in the Kerala state of India. In Ceylon (modern-day Sri Lanka) a native priest, Joseph Vaz, opened scores of churches and converted large numbers of his countrymen. The French Jesuit Alexander de Rhodes worked in Asia from 1623 to 1645. His greatest successes were in Vietnam. De Phodes put the Vietnamese language into a written form, translated religious materials into Vietnamese language into a written form, translated religious materials into Vietnamese, and trained catechists. His catechists also learned simple medical treatments. Thus they spread the Word of God and also served God's people. By 1650, thirty thousand Vietnamese were Catholic. De Rhodes and other Jesuits worked in Macau (muh-kow), China, and established the first Asian seminary in Ayutthaya (ah-yoo-teye-eh), Thailand, in 1665.

In Africa, the Capuchins had been working in Zaire and Angola for years. By 1700 an estimated five hundred thousand converts had been made. However, the slave trade and the instability brought about by fighting among colonizers harmed the missionary efforts. Nevertheless, French missionaries began work in Senegal in 1626 and in Madagascar in 1686.

During the 1600s, Spanish missionaries continued their efforts throughout the Americas and the Philippines. Because of the agreement between the Spanish king and the pope that allowed the king to appoint missionaries and oversee their work, Spanish missionaries were seen as both preachers and colonizers. Also, since the Spanish king forbade the training of native priests, the Church was seen as a foreign institution in which the local people would always be second-class members. Despite this problem, converts were drawn to the Church, and the faith took root.

The Spanish methods of missionary work conflicted sharply with the approaches taken by the Jesuits. The Spanish friars-Dominicans, Franciscans, and Augustinians-tried to get the local people to accept western culture and language, and to reject native customs and language. They believed that western, especially Spanish, culture was best and more Christian. The Jesuit missionaries, on the other hand, tried to live as the local people did, to use the language of those with whom they worked. The Jesuit brand of missionary work was typified by Matteo Ricci (see China Reverie) and others who worked in China. Because Chinese culture was ancient and very sophisticated, Ricci tried to make his way into Chinese society by adapting to Chinese culture. For instance, by 1660 the Mass was being said in Chinese, not Latin.

At first the Congregation for the Propagation of the Faith endorsed the Jesuit's approach. However, the Spanish friars could not accept the practice of saying the Mass in any language other than Latin and they raised objections with various popes. Finally, in 1704, Pope Clement XI banned the Chinese Mass and approved of the notion that people in missionary lands should adopt Western customs along with Christianity. This decision had far reaching effects. One immediate effect was that Emperor K'ang-his outlawed all Christian missionary work and threw almost all the Jesuits out of China. Understandably he found Clement's decision an insult to Chinese culture and to himself. Chinese Catholics felt abandoned; they were persecuted, and some who did not renounce their faith were executed as being traitors to China.

My good friend, Father Dennis Newton, SVD (Society of the Divine Word, Techny, Il.) wrote this article in the Divine Word Missionaries Magazine, Summer 2007, issue entitled "A Glimpse of India, Land and Languages." Here is that article.

"A Glimpse of India"
Land and Languages
Dennis Newton SVD

India is second only to China as the most popular country in the world with a population of over one billion people. While India is home for 16.7 percent of the world population, its land provides for only 2.4 percent. India is slightly more than a third of the size of the United States.

India won its independence in 1947 and it is the world's largest democracy. The country is divided into twenty-eight states and seven union territories. It has a federal form of government and a bicameral parliament.

India has a rich cultural heritage expressed in a wide variety of languages and literatures; arts and crafts; music, dance and festivals.

Although Hindi and English are the principal official languages of India, there are 22 officially recognized regional languages in the Constitution of India. Hindi is the first language of about a third of the population and many more people speak Hindi as a second language.

Religions

India, known as the land of spirituality and philosophy, is the birthplace of a number of world religions, among which are Hinduism, Jainism, Buddhism and Sikhism. Along with the religions that developed in India, there are non-Indian religions which claim followers. The largest non-Indian religions are Islam and Christianity. Today about 80 percent of the Indian population consists of Hindus; 13.4 percent Muslims and 2.34 percent Christians. It is estimated that about 70 percent of the Christians in India are Catholics.

Hindu society is highly structured according to a social order known as the "caste system." There are four main categories of castes (Varnas) including a category of out-castes, earlier called "untouchables" but now commonly referred to as Dalits. Within these broad categories, there are thousands of castes and sub-castes. Many of the problems of the Dalits are a result of the vested economic and political interests of those at the top of the social ladder. Dalits make up about 16 percent of the Indian population, and they are mostly landless agricultural laborers who are economically very poor, politically weak and socially marginalized. Tribals make up about 8 percent of the total Indian population, and nearly all of them live in rural areas.

Christianity in India

Christianity in India is as old as Christianity itself. According to tradition, it was Thomas, one of the twelve Apostles, who brought the faith to India. In 52 A.D., St. Thomas landed on the Malabar Coast of India (the present day Kerala). The Catholic Church in India is unique in its unfolding in three rites. Each of these rites has its own independent hierarchy. Two of the rites, with roots in Kerala State, constitute nearly 25 percent of the Indian church. These rites, both in union with Rome, are the Syro-Malabar Rite and the Syro-Malankara Rite. The Latin Rite Church in India traces its origin to Western missionaries who arrived in the 15th century. The Latin rite was bolstered in the 15th century with the arrival of St. Francis Xavier. During the 19th century many Tribals and Dalits converted to Catholicism.

Today's Situation

Historically, Hindus and Christians have lived in relative peace since the arrival of Christianity in India during the early part of the first millennium. In more contemporary periods, Hindu-Christian amity is sometimes challenged by partisan politics and extremism from both communities. There have been very strong moves to re-convert several Indian Christians back to Hinduism. As a response to aggressive missionary activity, three Indian states controlled by Hindu nationalist parties(Rajasthan, Madhya, Pradesh, and Tamil Nadu) have passed laws restricting or prohibiting conversion. This has created some resentment in the Indian Christian community.

After independence, the Indian government began to restrict the entry of foreign missionaries. This move resulted in a strong initiative to recruit and train indigenous, Indian vocations. There are 157 ecclesiastical units in India comprising 29 archdioceses and 128 dioceses. Of these, 127 are Latin Rite, 25 Syro-Malabar Rite and 5 Syro-Malankara Rite. The total number of diocesan priests is 14,000; priest-members of religious communities number 13,500. There are also 4.300 religious Brothers, and over 90,000 religious Sisters at present in India. With the steady growth of vocations in India, many religious orders are able to send missionaries to work outside of India. Divine Word Missionaries alone has sent almost 200 missionaries to 25 countries.

Despite the good work and social services offered by the Catholic Church, the growing atmosphere of Hindu fundamentalism has resulted in some problems for the Church. Work done among Tribals and Dalits is looked upon with some suspicion. Attacks on Christian institutions and property, the murder of priests, Sisters and lay people, the discrimination against Christians in public offices, and anti-missionary rhetoric have markedly increased in recent years.

The challenge for the Church in India is to uphold the sanctity, integrity and dignity of the life of all people: to hear the voices of those who are abused, of the vulnerable-women and children, and refugees, of unemployed youth and migrant workers; to assist those suffering and dying of HIV/AIDS and other diseases; to hear the faint voices of women and children who are trafficked, and to rescue the Falits and Tribals deprived of human dignity.

The following article from the same summer 2007 magazine was written by Father Richard Vaz S.V.D., and should broaden our understanding of the Tribal peoples.

"New Mission Among the Santal Tribe"

Driven by the charisma of the Society of the Divine Word, the India Eastern Province has set its feet among the Santal tribe in the Archdiocese of Kolkata in the state of West Bengal. Tribal peoples constitute 8.3 percent of India's total population-over 84 million people according to the 2001 census. Tribals are not part of the caste system; theirs is an egalitarian society.

The Santals are the third largest homogeneous tribal group of India. They have their own socio-political, economic and cultural systems to which they have sentimental and emotional links, and they practice their rituals religiously even today. They subsist primarily by rice farming. An important part of social life is music, dance and singing. Dances are linked with the fertility of the harvest, and they are performed separately by men and women before and after the rainy season, and between sowing and harvesting.

Most of the Santals live a life of abject poverty. The root cause of poverty is the exploitative tendency and the inadequate socio-political and economic structures. Consequent upon these factors is dispossession of basic life sustaining resources: land, forest and waters, as well as cultures and values. Government policies on forest reserves have affected tribal peoples profoundly.

The mission for the Divine Word Missionaries is the holistic uplifting of the entire tribal community. Santals have shown keener interest in Christianity than in any other religion, and a greater desire to embrace Christianity than to accept any other faith. For this reason, two Divine Word Missionaries have been sent to Bezda, the place where they hope to set up a mission station. As one of the missionaries writes: Our immediate concern will be to provide the children with basic education, to set up programs for sustained livelihoods, and to empower the poor, especially the women, with the rights and dignity of life. We shall assume a role of advocacy and animation, and prevent people from unsafe migration, trafficking and exploitation by the agents and middlemen who work for contractors of flesh trade.

These projects demand the setting up of a basic infra-structure: a school, a hostel for children, a health center, a vocational training center. The missionaries count on the support of friends, and invite them to share the mission of building up a healthy human community of the Santal tribe at Bezda.

Both the history of the Taj Mahal and India's peaceful fight for independence from England go beyond the scope of this reverie. However, most of us remember watching India's valiant struggle for independence in the Movietone News shown between the double-features in our local movie theaters in the 1940s. Some of us might remember reading about the India's struggle in our local newspapers during these same years and how we rejoiced with India when they finally attained their independence on August 15, 1947! But in all of the movies and newspapers two names always stood out (1) Mahatma (1869-1948) The Hindu nationalist leader, and (2) Jawaharlal Nehru (born in 1880), an Indian nationalist, who was elected the first Prime Minister of the Dominion of India on August 15, 1947; two very great men of the 20th century!! But there is another name that became "one of the most compelling Christian witnesses of the twentieth century" and most certainly be included in this reverie. This great woman once said "to show great love for God and our neighbor we need not do great things. It is how much love we put in the doing that makes our offering something beautiful for God." By now you have guessed her name: Mother Teresa of Calcutta! Let us read what my friend, Robert Ellsberg, wrote about her.

Mother Teresa of Calcutta was the founder of the Missionaries of Charity (1910-1997). On September 10, 1946, the woman who would become Mother Teresa was traveling on a train to Darjeeling, a hill station in the Himalayas. At the time she was simply Sister Agnes, a 36-year-old Loreto Sister of Albanian extraction, who had spent the past twenty years teaching in her order's schools in India. Though she was a devoted nun, beloved by her mostly middle-class students, there was nothing to suggest that she would one day be regarded as one of the most compelling Christian witnesses of the twentieth century. But on this day she received "a call within a call." God, she suddenly felt, wanted something more from her: "He wanted me to be poor with the poor and to love Him in the distressing disguise of the poorest of the poor."

So, with the permission of her congregation, she left her convent. In place of her traditional religious habit she donned a simple white sari with blue border and went out to seek Jesus in the desperate byways of Calcutta. Eventually she was joined by others—including many of her former students. They became the Missionaries of Charity. And she became Mother Teresa.

With time Mother Teresa would establish centers of service around the globe for the sick, the homeless, the unwanted. But she was particularly identified with her home for the dying in Calcutta. There, destitute and dying men and women, gathered off the streets of the city, were welcomed to receive loving care and respect until they died. Those who had lived like "animals in the gutter" were enable, in Mother Teresa's home, to "die like angels"—knowing that they were truly valued and loved as precious children of God.

It was not Mother Teresa's way to change social structures. "We are not social workers," she said, but "contemplatives in the heart of the world for we are touching the body of Christ twenty-four hours a day." It was this mystical insight, which she obviously lived, that made Mother Teresa such a widely inspiring figure. She did not simply practice charity; she embodied it.

> God has identified himself with the hungry, the sick, the naked, the homeless; hunger, not only for bread, but for love, for care, to be somebody to someone; nakedness, not of clothing only, but nakedness of that compassion that very few people give to the unknown; homelessness, not only just for a shelter made of stone, but that homelessness that comes from having no one to call your own.

For many years Mother Teresa toiled in obscurity. But eventually she was "discovered: by the world. She became the subject of documentary films and biographies; she received honorary degrees from prestigious universities and countless honors, including the Nobel Peace Prize for 1979. Widely regarded as a "living saint," she nevertheless remained remarkably unburdened by such adulation. Nor did she have any exalted sense of her own vocation. "We can do no great things," she said, "only small things with great love." Often when people begged to join her in her "wonderful work" in Calcutta she would respond gently but firmly: "Find your own Calcutta!" As she explained,

> Don't search for God in far lands—he is not there. He is close to you, He is with you. Just keep the lamp burning and you will always see him. Watch and pray. Keep kindling the lamp and you will see his love and you will see how sweet is the Lord you love.

In later life Mother Teresa traveled widely around the world. In the affluent West she had no trouble finding poverty—both the material kind and a no less destructive impoverishment of the spirit. The answer in both cases was love, a love that would begin with persons and ultimately transform the world. But before we tried to love the entire world, we should start by trying to love one other person—someone apparently unlovable, unwanted, or rejected. "You can save only one at a time. We can love only one at a time." That, she believed, is what we were put on earth to do: "Something beautiful for God." Mother Teresa died on September 5, 1997.

Albert A. Hoffman, Jr.

My prediction is that in the years to come Mother Teresa will be recognized as a prophetess, she along with John Paul II will be canonized as saint' and both will be judged as the two most holy and outstanding human beings of the twentieth century!

We will end this reverie with the great English writer, Rudyard Kipling, born in 1865 and died in 1936, eleven years before India obtained its independence. But in the many words he penned you can feel his great respect he had for the Indian people, the dignity they possessed and the great injustice the English government committed in denying India its freedom. He expressed this sentiment shared by most English citizens when he wrote his great and poignant poem GUNGA DIN!

You may talk o'gin an' beer
When you're quartered safe out 'ere,
An' you're sent to penny—fights an' Aldershot it;
But if it comes to slaughter
You will do your work on water,
An' you'll lick the bloomin' boots of 'im that's got it.
Now in Injia's sunny clime,
Where I used to spend my time
a—servin' of 'Er Majesty the Queen,
of all them black-faced crew
the finest man I knew
was our regimental bhisti, Gunga Din.
It was "Din! Din! Din!
You limping lump o' brick-dust, Gunga Din!
Hi! Slippy hitherao!
Water, get it! Panee Lao!
You squidgy-nosed old idol, Gunga Din!"

The uniform 'e wore
Was nothin' much before,
An' rather less than 'arf o' that be'ind,
For a twisty piece o'rag
An' a goatskin water-bag
Was all the field-equipment 'e could find.
When the sweatin' troop-train lay
In a sidin through the day,
Where the 'eat would make your bloomin' eyebrows crawl,
We shouted "Harry By!"
Till our throats were bricky-dry,
Then we wopped 'im 'cause 'e couldn't serve us all.

It was "Din! Din! Din!
You 'eathen, where the mischief 'ave you been?
You put some juldee in it,
Or I'll marrow you this minute,
If you don't fill up my helmet, Gunga Din!"

'E would dot an' carry one
Till the longest day was done,
An' 'e didn't seem to know the use o' fear.
If we charged or broke or cut,
You could bet your bloomin' nut,
'E'd be waitin' fifty paces right flank rear.
With 'is mussick on 'is back,
'E would skip with our attack,
An' watch us till the bugles made "Retire."
An' for all 'is dirty 'ide,
'E was white, clear white, inside
When 'e went to tend the wounded under fire!

\It was "Din! Din! Din!"
So I'll meet 'im later on
In the place where 'e is gone—
Where it's always double drill and no canteen;
'E'll be squattin' on the coals
Givin' drink to pore damned souls,
An' I'll get a swig in Hell from Gunga Din!

Din! Din! Din!
You Lazarushian-leather Gunga Din!
Tho' I've belted you an' flayed you,
By the livin' Gawd that made you,
You're a better man than I am, Gunga Din!

Thank you, Mr. Rudyard Kipling! In your own way you helped bring about the independence of India.

Bert Hoffman

NATIONS AND THE CATHOLIC CHURCH—A REVERIE

Well, gentle readers, we come to the last month of our International Year and to our last Reverie, it was quite a journey!! This is Webster's definition of Reverie and best defines my reveries: State of being lost in thought; also, a musing. Incidentally, most of what I intend to write in this final reverie I could not have written one year ago. These thoughts slowly developed out of the first eleven chapters. So, please be patient, understanding and forgiving as you read on.

God is eternal—God had no beginning and will have no end. Out of love he created everything out of nothing. He created all the angels, trillions and trillions of them. The highest and wisest angel was Lucifer aka Satan, the devil, the father of lies, the dragon. From his pride came his disobedience to God, leading to death and this is how evil and hell came into existence. Perhaps up to one third of the angels followed his example, they are called demons. They hate God, His creation and the human beings He created.

"War broke out in heaven; Michael and his angels battled against the dragon. The dragon and its angels fought back, but they did not prevail and there was no longer any place for them in heaven. The huge dragon, the ancient serpent, who is called the devil or satan, who deceived the whole world, was thrown down to earth, and its angels were thrown down with it." (Revelation) This should never be forgotten, if it is forgotten, we will never understand how so much evil that we see all around us came into existence. Yes, we are in continuous spiritual warfare with the devil and the forces of evil. Our strongest weapon in this battle is prayer.

Every human being receives an individual guardian angel when he/she is conceived, this is a good angel, your messenger from God, who is with you all your life.

> Angel of God, my guardian dear
> To whom His love commits me here
> Ever this day be at my side
> To light, to guard
> To rule and guide. Amen

Three archangels, Sts. Michael, Gabriel and Raphael, are commemorated on their feast day, September 29. They represent the primary roles of angels. Michael is a warrior against evil, "captain of the heavenly host" and special protector of Israel and of the church. Gabriel is a messenger who announced the Messiah's coming and the births of John the Baptist and Jesus. Raphael served as a guardian angel protecting Tobiah on his journey. Like them, may we learn that we are sent to become warriors against evil, announcers of good news and guardians of those who need help. St. Hildegard of Bingen wrote "to the Trinity be praise! God is music, God is life that nurtures every creature in its kind. Our God is the song of the angel throng and the splendor of secret ways hid from all mankind. But God our life is the life of all."

Scientists have estimated the age of the universe to be about 19 billion years old. It was created out of nothing by Almight God. The earth as we know it now is estimated to be about 4 1/2 billion years old and our first parents Adam and Eve came into existence about 2 million years ago. This primeval history can be read in the first 11 chapters of Genesis, the first book of the bible. God's entry into the history of the human race can be read in chapters 12 of Genesis and continues to the end of the 73 books of the Catholic Bible. All creation follows the laws of the nature God gave them, the natural law. Only human beings were created in the image and likeness of God, that is, they have an intellect, a will, a memory and an immortal soul that is given to them at the moment of conception and which will never die but which will leave their body at the moment of death. Adam and Eve lived in the garden of Eden but told not to eat the forbidden fruit of the tree of life. They could think, they could reason, they had complete control of their bodies, they could remember, they had a free will, they could choose, and they would not die. Now, enter the serpent, the father of lies, who convinced them they would become like God if they ate the forbidden fruit. They believed the serpent and ate the forbidden fruit, and committed the original sin, and so for the first time evil crept into the world (sin, sickness and death), the gates of heaven were closed to them and to all their offspring. They needed a savior, a redeemer, a messiah. Since the original sin was against God, only a divine person could redeem the world and reopen the gates of heaven. But God so loved the world that He gave His only Son, so that everyone who believes in Him may not die but have eternal life. He sent the Messiah, Jesus Christ, to redeem the world which he did by His passion, death and resurrection.

One more biblical story should be told concerning the Catholic Church before moving on. One day near the town of Caesarea Philippi, Jesus asked his disciples "who do people say I am? Who do you say I am?" Simon Peter answered, "You are the Messiah, the Son of the living God." Jesus answered "good for you, Simon, son of John! For this truth did not come to you from any human being, but it was given to you directly by my Father in heaven. And so I tell you, Peter: you are a rock, and on this rock foundation I will build My church, and not even death will ever be able to overcome it. I will give you the keys of the kingdom of heaven, what you prohibit on earth will be prohibited in heaven, and what you permit on earth will be permitted in heaven." Note all verbs are singular. Peter was the first pope, the vicar (a deputy) of Christ on earth, the pope is the supreme head over the universal church, in other words, the full, supreme, immediate and universal authority which was only given to Peter and not to the other apostles. That's why the successors of Peter, the pope, has more authority in the church than the successors of the apostles—the bishops. There has been a continuous line of 266 popes from St. Peter to Benedict XVI (2008).

In reading these reveries, one can not fail to notice and appreciate the impact the Catholic Church had on these eleven nations and by extension, on the entire world; especially in the battles between good and evil. The Catholic Church was always on the side of good.

> Let us rejoice in the Lord! Let us join with the angels
> In joyful praise to the Son of God. O God, You have
> Created all nations and You are their salvation.
> Grant us strength that we may remain faithful to your
> Commandments even unto death.

"Whoever acknowledges Me before the world, I will acknowledge before My Father in heaven. The most necessary virtue of all is love." (St. Anthony Mary Claret)

> "To govern one's passions is to become master
> Of one's world. We must either command them
> Or be enslaved by them. It is better to be a
> Hammer than an anvil." (St. Dominic)

"People aspire to what is beautiful and love it. But what is beautiful is also good. God is good. Every one looks for the good, therefore everyone looks for God." (St. Basil the Great)

And now, gentle readers, back to the impact the Catholic Church had on the world. I have selected appropriate passages from two sources that somehow relate to the eleven reveries in many and varied ways, at least I hope they do but you may have to use your imagination to see how. The two sources are

1. "How the Catholic church built western civilization" by Thomas Woods, Professor of History, State University of New York. He examines the ways in which the highly influential church affected economics, literature, education, and a variety of aspects of society throughout

centuries of history. Woods argues that the Catholic church has had a monumental impact on the development of western civilization as a whole. What role will the Catholic Church play in the coming century? How has it maintained its influence over such a long period of time, despite the forces of war, revolution and change?
2. Roman Catholic Church; Wikipedia, The Free Encyclopedia (*HTTP://EN.WIKIPEDIA.ORG/WIA/ROMANCATHOLIC* CHURCH)

Manitowoc, Wis.: There is a popular misconception that the Catholic Church actively discouraged science from being studied or pursued. Please address this misconception. Thank you.

Thomas Woods: I make two main points in my science chapter: 1.) That certain Catholic theological ideas lent themselves to the development of science; and 2.) That Catholic priests, particularly the Jesuits, were unknown pioneers in science. How many people know 35 craters on the moon are names for Jesuit scientists? Or that the Jesuits brought Western science to India, China, etc.? Or that the first person to measure the rate of acceleration of a freely-falling body was a Jesuit? And so on. Thus David Lindberg, Edward Grant, and other historians of science say just the opposite: it was the atmosphere of scholarly exchange and the emphasis on reason that developed in the medieval university—with the blessing and encouragement of the church—that made possible the kind of intellectual milieu in which the Scientific Revolution could arise. I think we all have certain misconceptions from our K-12 education—indeed even our college education—that thinks the Church is responsible only for the Inquisition and Galileo. This is really neither reasonable nor fair. As for the Holocaust, why did Jews—at the time—praise Pope Pius XII, and why is all the bitterness and nastiness toward him coming the further away in time we get from the event?

What's interesting about this question is that here we have yet another area in which modern scholars are taking another look at the record and finding the Church to have pioneered. Joseph Schumpeter, one of the 20th century's great economists, says the 16th-century Scholastics were the founders of modern scientific economics. Economics didn't all emerge from Adam Smith's brain in the 18th century. Alejandro Chafuen shows in his great book Faith and Liberty just how sympathetic to the free market these 16th-century Catholic theologians were. I take up this point in my own defense of the market—a book of mine called "The Church and the Market: A Catholic Defense of the Free Economy."

That's the point of my book. When you look at the distinctive features of Western civilization, we are deeply indebted to the Church for a great many of them. Thus, for instance, even W.E.H. Lecky, one of the Church's great 19th-century opponents, admitted that the ancient world had nothing even approaching the Church's institutionalized care for widows, orphans, and the sick. The whole ethos of Catholic charity was leagues above that of the ancient world. The Church's insistence on the sacredness of human life meant that she had to work against gladiatorial contests, which trivialized human life, and against the practice of infanticide.

As for those who indict the Church for Spanish conquests in the new World. The origins of international law—the idea that states are morally answerable to absolute standards—developed precisely because priest—theologians in Spanish universities were so appalled by their countrymen's behavior. This is something new under the sun: the idea that there exists an absolute moral standard that applies to my own people as well as to others, and by which I may render a negative moral judgment on my own people. Attila the Hun never did that.

Likewise, everyone thinks the Middle Ages were a time of ignorance and stupidity. No medieval scholar thinks so. But it takes a long, long time sometimes for the conclusions of scholars to reach the general public. In the meantime, the Church's image suffers. One way she can improve that image is through education, of course, and my book is a contribution to that project. Another way is to deal much more swiftly and decisively against frankly evil people in the church. This timidity about the use of ecclesiastical discipline has got to stop. But finally, she can keep doing her good works: we'll never know all the stories of conversions that occurred in AIDS care centers when the person caring for these dying people was so often a nun, smiling at them and comforting them. There's nothing evil about that.

Pope John Paul II wrote a letter to artists toward the end of his pontificate that you might look at. In a nutshell, the church is fully aware of the role and importance of the arts—the Counter Reformation certainly showed that. I think what is happening is this. During the Renaissance but much more clearly with Romanticism, there began a tendency for the artist to emphasize his expression of himself, even more than the thing he was reproducing. Self-expression for the Romantics was the heart of the arts. To a degree this is all well and good, but it can easily degenerate into outright narcissism. You now have a world of modern art that is simply impossible to parody. The idea that as an artist I am going to produce something beautiful—something greater than and outside of myself—for your contemplation is laughed at now.

Notre Dame is one place, at least in architecture, where this kind of narcissism/nihilism is being addressed. But the Church in some cases has her own people to blame: Who's responsible for all these hideous modern churches, that have all the warmth of an insane asylum?

It was largely under the influence of the Church in the early to high Middle Ages that trials by ordeal (common in Germanic folk law) began to be replaced by rational procedures and rules of evidence; the Church's canon law was the model here. Before the twelfth century was out you have some of the great universities forming—Paris, Oxford, Cambridge, Bologna. This is an entirely new development in the world. (Yes, there were schools, but not with all the features of the university.) Lindberg, in "The Beginnings of Western Science", notes that contrary to what people think, professors in these universities had an enormous range of intellectual freedom. This was protected by the Church; it was the popes who, in a world of conflicting jurisdictions, consistently intervened on behalf of the university and its rights.

The Church has always recognized a hierarchy of reasons for which people do good. Some people do good simply out of fear of hell. For some, that's the only motivation that can reach them, but the Church considers this by far the lowest rationale. For others it's the desire for heaven. But for those with the best spiritual formation, and those the Church recommends to the world, it is a pure love for God that motivates them. Plus, in real life it is not so easy to separate out the precise motivations people have at any one time. Surely Mother Teresa's Missionaries of Charity hope to go to heaven, but can that really be the full explanation for what they're doing? They could go to heaven working in an air-conditioned office, too. Look into their eyes and see if you see faces who merely seek a reward. Tell me if you don't see something much deeper and more profound.

I think the Church in the United States has, unfortunately, suffered from some fairly abysmal leadership these past several decades. Bishop Fabian Bruskewitz got into some trouble several years ago when he said essentially that—the American episcopate is sorely lacking. But His Excellency was surely on to something. This poor leadership, in some cases even cowardice, has contributed to the state of the Church in America today. Yet one can never say the Church doesn't need this or that place. She needs every place—"Catholic," after all, means universal. But given the growing numbers of Catholics elsewhere in the world, she certainly needs to concern herself less (if she ever did at all) with opinion polls of American Catholics that seems to demand this or that accommodation to the modern world. Heck, can't we have one organization that's a little skeptical of the modern world?

There have always been licit differences in worship and in traditions of spirituality within the Church—the Dominicans differ from the Trappists, for instance, who differ from the Franciscans. There have even been multiple liturgical rites used. The Dominicans, for instance, used to have their own rite. There are over a dozen approved Eastern rites. So to some extent, this is all well and good. The problem comes when differences arise that—to borrow some Scholastic terminology—are substantial rather than accidental. Right now the rite of Mass in use throughout the Roman Rite of the Church is yielding liturgies so radically at odds with one another—liturgies done within the same rite, the same liturgical books—as to throw the universal Church into confusion. Erroneous teachings are being spread. A self-centered style of worship is becoming fashionable. This is indeed a serious problem. I am hopeful that the new Pope, who has written at great length and with much eloquence on the liturgy, will try to reverse this problem. He has said many times that he wants the traditional rite of Mass, before the changes of 1969-70, made much more widely available. That Mass produced great saints and served as a great unifier. It can do so again. Thank you. I myself am a convert. I found that the more I read, the more fascinated and impressed I became. No, the church isn't perfect—what institution staffed by human beings is? Yes, evil has at times been done in her name. But to stop there is to be gratuitously unfair.

It's interesting, though: we don't realize just what a staggering undertaking the Catholic school system was. Here's a largely immigrant population, barely getting their bearings over here, and they're now going to erect an entire school system. Archbishop John Ireland wondered if it was sapping too much energy and was simply not possible. But the overwhelming consensus was that a specifically Catholic education was so important to the formation of good souls that no sacrifice—within reason—was too great. Catholic teachings stress forgiveness, doing good for others, especially those most in need, and the sanctity of life. Catholics were pacifists in the earliest days of the Church, as witnessed by the fact that Christians were forbidden to join the Roman Army. This was part of the cause of their political persecution in the empire. Today, however, only some Catholics hold that position, with various analysis of the "just war theory" more widely held. It should be noted that the purpose of the Catholic "just war" criteria is to prevent and limit war rather than to justify it.

Capital punishment, though it has not been absolutely condemned by the Church, has come under increasing criticism by theologians and Church leaders. Pope John Paul II, for instance, opposed capital punishment in all instances as being immoral, because there are other options for punishment and deterrence in the modern world. He, along with most other modern Catholic theologians, held that if capital punishment was ever moral—a position some dispute—it would only be justifiable when there was no other option for the protection of the lives of others. After four years of consultations with the world's Catholic bishops, John Paul II wrote that execution is only appropriate "in cases of absolute necessity: in other words, when it would not be possible otherwise to defend society. Today however, as a result of steady improvements in the organization of the penal system, such cases are very rare, if not practically non-existent." This position is also held today by Avery Cardinal Dulles, Msgr. William Smith, Germain Grisez and other Catholic moral theologians.

Likewise, the great variety of Catholic spirituality enables individual Catholics to pray privately in many different ways. The fourth and last part of the Catechism thus summarized the Catholic's response to the mystery of faith: "This mystery, then, requires that the faithful believe in it, that they celebrate it, and that they live from it in a vital and personal relationship with the living and true God. This relationship is prayer." All baptized members of the Catholic Church are called faithful, truly equal in dignity and in the work to build the Church.

All are called to share in Christ's priestly, prophetic, and royal office. While a certain percentage of the faithful perform roles related to serving the ministerial priesthood (hierarchy) and giving eschatological witness (consecrated life), the great majority of the faithful perform a specific role of exercising the three offices of Christ by "engaging in temporal affairs and directing them according to God's will . . . to illuminate and order all temporal things." These are the laity, whom John Paul II urged in *Christifideles laici* "to take an active, conscientious and responsible part in the mission of the Church," for they not only belong to the Church, but *"are the Church."* Equipped with the common priesthood in baptism, these ordinary Catholics—e.g., mothers, farmers, businessmen, writers, politicians—are to take initiative in "discovering or inventing the means for permeating social, political, and economic realities with the demands of Christian doctrine and life." They exercise the common, baptism-based *priestly office* by offering their works as spiritual sacrifices, the *prophetic office* by their word and testimony of life in the ordinary circumstances of the world, and the *kingly office* by self-mastery and conforming worldly institutions to the norms of justice. This theology of the laity, called a "characteristic mark" of Vatican II by Paul VI and John Paul II, was complemented, and in some cases influenced, by the rise of many lay ecclesial movements and structures in the 20th century: examples are Focolare, Neocatechumenal Way, Communion and Liberation, and the personal prelature of Opus Dei.

Many enlightenment philosophers perceived the Church's doctrines as superstitious and hindering the progress of civilization. In the most famous instance, many criticized it for the 1633 trial of Galileo Galilei, in which the Church condemned his advancement of the heliocentric system of Catholic priest Nicolaus Copernicus, in favour of a geocentric system. Pope John Paul II publicly apologized for the Church's actions in that trial on 31 October 1992. An abstract of the acts of the process against Galileo is available at the Vatican Secret Archives, which reproduces part of it on its website. Recently, the Church is criticized for its opposition to scientific research in fields such as embryonic stem cell research, which the Church teaches would cause the utilitarian destruction of a human being, or simply put, an act of murder. The Church argues that advances in medicine can come without the destruction of human embryos; for example, in the use of adult or umbilical stem cells in place of embryonic stem cells.

Historians of science including non-Catholics such as J.L. Heilbron, Alistair Cameron Crombie, David Lindberg, Edward Grant, Thomas Goldstein, and Ted Davis have been revising the common notion—the product of black legends say some—that the Church has had a negative influence in the development of civilization. They argue that not only did the monks save and cultivate the remnants of ancient civilization during the barbarian invasions, but the Church promoted learning and science through its sponsorship of many universities which, under its leadership, grew rapidly in Europe in the 11th and 12th centuries. St. Thomas Aquinas, the Church's "model theologian," not only argued that reason is in harmony with faith, he even recognized that reason can contribute to understanding revelation, and so encouraged intellectual development. The Church's priest—scientists, many of whom were Jesuits, were the leading lights in astronomy, genetics, geomagnetism, meteorology, seismology, and solar physics, becoming the "fathers" of these sciences. It is important to remark names of important churchmen such as the Agustinian abbot Gregor Mendel (pioneer in the study of genetics) and Belgian priest Georges Lemaitre (the first to propose the Big Bang theory). John Cardinal Newman used to say in the nineteenth century that those who attack the Church can only point to the Galileo case, which to many historians does not prove the Church's opposition to science since many of the churchmen at that time were encouraged by the Church to continue their research.

While some critics accuse members of the Catholic Church of destroying the art of some of the colonized natives, several historians credit the Catholic Church for the brilliance and magnificence of Western art. They refer to the Church's fight against iconoclasm, a movement against visual representations of the divine, its insistence on building structures befitting worship, Augustine's repeated reference to Wisdom 11:20 (God "ordered all things by measure and number and weight") which led to the geometric constructions of Gothic architecture, the scholastics' coherent intellectually systems called the Summa Theologiae which influenced the intellectually consistent writings of Dante, its creation and sacramental theology which has developed a Catholic imagination influencing writers such as J.R.R. Tolkien and William Shakespeare, and lastly, the patronage of the Renaissance popes for the great works of Catholic artists such as Michelangelo, Raphael, Bernini, Borromini and Leonardo da Vinci.

Francisco de Vitoria, a disciple of Thomas Aquinas and a Catholic thinker who studied the issue regarding the human rights of colonized natives, is recognized by the United Nations as a father of international law, and now also by historians of economics and democracy as a leading light for the West's democracy and rapid economic development. Joseph Schumpeter, an economist of the twentieth century, referring to the scholastics, wrote, "it is they who come nearer than does any other group to having been the 'founders' of scientific economics." Other economists and historians, such as Raymond de Roover, Marjorie Grice-Hutchinson, and Alejandro Chafuen, have also made similar statements. Historian Paul Legutko of Stanford University said the Catholic Church is "at the center of the development of the values, ideas, science, laws, and institutions which constitute what we call Western civilization."

While it is criticized in many places, the Catholic Church also has contributed much to society through its Social Doctrine which has guided leaders to promote social justice and by setting up the hospital system in Medieval Europe, a system which was different from the merely reciprocal hospitality of the Greeks and family-based obligations of the Romans. These hospitals were established to cater to "particular social groups marginalized by poverty, sickness, and age," according to historian of hospitals, Guenter Risse. James Joseph Walsh wrote the following about the Catholic Church's contribution to the hospital system:

> During the thirteenth century an immense number of (these) hospitals were built. The Italian cities were the leaders of the movement. Milan had no less than a dozen hospitals and Florence before the end of the Fourteenth century had some thirty hospitals. Some of these were very beautiful buildings. At Milan a portion of the general hospital was designed by Bramante and another part of it by Michelangelo. The Hospital of the innocents in Florence for foundlings was an architectural gem. The Hospital of Sienna, built in honor of St. Catherine, has been famous ever since. Everywhere throughout Europe this hospital movement spread. Virchow, the great German pathologist, in an article on hospitals, showed that every city of Germany of five thousand inhabitants had its hospital. He traced all of this hospital movement to Pope Innocent III, and though he was least papistically inclined, Virchow did not hesitate to give extremely high praise to this pontiff for all that he had accomplished for the benefit of children and suffering mankind.

The beauty and efficiency of the Italian hospitals inspired even some who were otherwise critical of the Church. The German historian Ludwig von Pastor recounts the words of Martin Luther who, while journeying to Rome in the winter of 1510-1511, had occasion to visit some of these hospitals:

> In Italy, he remarks, the hospitals are handsomely built, and admirably provided with excellent food and drink, careful attendants and learned physicians. The beds and bedding are clean, and the walls are covered with paintings. When a patient is brought in, his clothes are removed in the presence of a notary who makes a faithful inventory of them, and they are kept safely. A white smock is put on him and he is laid on a comfortable bed, with clean linen. Presently two doctors come to him, and servants bring him food and drink in clean glasses, showing him all possible attention.

The Catholic Church as opus proprium, says Benedict XVI in Deus Caritas Est, has conducted throughout the centuries from its very beginning and continues to conduct many charitable services—hospitals, schools, poverty alleviation programs, among others.

Since both Popes, John Paul II and Benedict XVI, have both hinted that the world is in its final confrontation between good and evil, between Christ and the Devil, between love and hate, and between truth and lies. Even in our lifetime we have witnessed the battle between Christianity and Secular Humanism. The adjective secular pertains to the worldly or temporal as distinguished from the spiritual or eternal specifically: a.) not under Church control; non ecclesiastical, civil, as secular courts or education b.) not sacred; profane, as secular music. Humanism pertains to human nature; humanity; a mode or attitude of thought or action centering upon distinctively human interests or ideals. Humanitarianism is the tenet denying the divinity of Christ. Secular Humanism holds that man is the measure of all things, Christianity holds that God is the measure of all things (the secular world versus the Catholic Faith). The secular world, however, is attracted to Catholic Art, because it is so good, that is, its truth, justice, beauty and goodness.

This is verified by the millions of people around the world that traveled any distance to view the "Passion of Christ" by Mel Gibson! They want to live the life the Lord intends them to live! Art must reflect God, must motivate us to spiritual thoughts, if it doesn't do this it is not art but pornography.

> "The good Lord has worked and still works daily that we may achieve the glory of being fashioned as God, as long as we follow the example of our fashioning here in Christ." (St. Paulinus of Nola)

"To the Trinity be praise! God is music, God is life that nurtures every creature in its kind. Our God is the song of the angel throng and the splendor of secret ways hid from all mankind. But God our life is the life of all." (St. Hildegard of Bingen)

> "I would advise those who practice, especially at first, to cultivate the friendship and company of others who are working in the same way. This is a most important thing, because we can help one another by our prayers, and all the more so because it may bring us even greater benefits." (St. Teresa of Avila)

Prayer to St. Michael the Archangel

St. Michael the Archangel, defend us in the day of battle; be our safeguard against the wiles and wickedness of the devil. May God rebuke him, we humbly pray, and do thou, O Prince of the heavenly host, by the power of God cast into Hell Satan and all the other evil spirits, who prowl through the world, seeking the ruin of souls.

Bert Hoffman

Addendum One—December Reverie

Section 8 of the Second Vatican Council's decree on the church, Lumen Gentium, states that "the one Church of Christ which in the creed is professed as one, holy, catholic and apostolic subsists" in the Catholic Church, which is governed by the successor of Peter and by the bishops in communion with him." (The term successor of Peter refers in Catholic understanding to the Bishop of Rome, the Pope.) The four attributes or marks are introduced and explained in the catechism of the Catholic Church as follows:

> The church is one because of her source: "the highest exemplar and source of this mystery is the unity, in the Trinity of Persons, of one God, the Father, the Son in the Holy Spirit." The church is one because of her founder: for "the word made flesh, the Prince of peace, reconciled all men to God by the cross, restoring the unity of all in one people and one body." (paragraph8 pg. 13)

"The church is held, as a matter of faith, to be unfailingly holy. This is because Christ, the Son of God, who with the Father and the Spirit is hailed as 'alone holy,' loved the church as His bride, giving Himself up for her so as to sanctify her; he joined her to himself as his body and endowed her with the gift of the Holy Spirit for the glory of God." The church, then, is "the holy people of God."

The church is Catholic. The word "catholic" means "universal," in the sense of "according to the totality" or "in keeping with the whole." The church is catholic in a double sense:

> First, the church is catholic because Christ is present in her. "Where there is Christ Jesus, there is the Catholic church." In her subsists the fullness of Christ's body united with its head; this implies that she receives from Him "the fullness of the means of salvation" which He has willed: correct and complete confession of faith, full sacramental life, and ordained ministry in apostolic succession. The church was, in this fundamental sense, catholic on the day of Pentecost and will always be so until the day of the Parousia, the second coming of Jesus Christ.

Secondly, the church is catholic because she has been sent out by Christ on a mission to the whole of the human race. All men are called to belong to the new people of God. This people, therefore, while remaining one and only one, is to be spread throughout the whole world and to all ages in order that the design of God's will may be fulfilled: He made human nature one in the beginning and has decreed that all His children who were scattered should be finally gathered together as one. The character of universality which adorns the people of God is a gift from the Lord Himself whereby the Catholic Church ceaselessly and efficaciously seeks for the return of all humanity and all its goods, under Christ the head in the unity of His Spirit. (Paragraph 830, 831)

The church is apostolic because she is founded on the apostles, in three ways:

- she was and remains built on "the foundation of the apostles, "the witnesses chosen and sent on mission by Christ Himself;
- with the help of the Spirit dwelling in her, the church keeps and hands on the teaching, the "good deposit," the salutary words she has heard from the apostles;
- she continues to be taught, sanctified, and guided by the apostles until Christ's return, through their successors in pastoral office: the college of bishops, "assisted by priests, in union with the successor of Peter, the church's supreme pastor."

> You are the eternal Shepherd who never leaves His
> Flock untended.
> Through the apostles you watch over us and protect
> Us always.
> You made them shepherds of the flock to share in the
> Work of Your Son.

Addendum two to the December Reverie 2007

After rereading all the monthly reveries, I slowly recognized that I was unknowingly answering the question I posed in the forward of this book: "What am I talking about, who knows?" The answer to that question is the Catholic Church, especially in its bibles. I'm talking about truth and the truth is Jesus Christ. Jesus tells the truth about good and evil, the spiritual warfare between the forces of good against the forces of evil, especially against the devil and his demons. Why not read and ponder what Jesus said about good and evil? Why not begin with Chapter 8; vs 26-38, of the Gospel of St. Luke, "Jesus heals a man with demons": Jesus and His disciples sailed on over to the territory of Gerasa, which is across the lake from Galilee. As Jesus stepped ashore, He was met by a man from the town who had demons in him. For a long time this man had gone without clothes and would not stay at home, but spent his time in the burial caves. When he saw Jesus, he gave a loud cry, threw himself down at His feet, and shouted, "Jesus, Son of the Most High God! What do you want with me? I beg you, don't punish me!" He said this because Jesus had ordered the evil spirit to go out of him. Many times it had seized him, and even though he was kept a prisoner, his hands and feet tied with chains, he would break the chains and be driven by the demon out into the desert. Jesus asked him, "what is your name?" "My name is "Legion," he answered—because many demons had gone into him. The demons begged Jesus not to send them into the abyss. There was a large herd of pigs near by, feeding on a hillside. So the demons begged Jesus to let them go into the pigs, and He let them. They went out of the man and into the pigs. The whole herd rushed down the side of the cliff into the lake and was drowned. The men who had been taking care of the pigs saw what happened, so they ran off and spread the news to the town and among the farms. People went out to see what had happened, and when they came to Jesus, they found the man from whom the demons had gone out sitting at the feet of Jesus, clothed and in his right mind, and they were all afraid. Those who had seen it told the people how the man had been cured. Then all the people from that territory asked Jesus to go away, because they were terribly afraid. So Jesus got into the boat and left. The man from whom the demons had gone out begged Jesus, "Let me go with You." But Jesus sent him away, saying, "go back home and tell what God has done for you." The man went through the town, telling what Jesus had done for him.

Addendum three to the December Reverie 2007

The day of the Lord is coming. The Lord will come again as sure as you are reading these words.

The prophet Malachi wrote in the fifth century, B.C.: "The Lord Almighty says, the day is coming when all proud and evil people will burn like straw. On that day they will burn up, and there will be nothing left of them. But for you who obey Me, My saving power will rise on you like the sun and bring healing like the sun's rays. You will be as free and happy as calves let out of a stall. On the day when I act, you will overcome the wicked, and they will be like dust under your feet." (4:1-3)

The gospel writer, St. Luke, writes in chapter 21 about the end of the world with the second coming of Jesus Christ. "His disciples asked Jesus 'teacher, when will this happen? And what sign will there be when all these things are about to happen?' He answered, 'see that you not be deceived, for many will come in my name, saying, 'I am He,' and 'the time has come.' Do not follow them! When you hear of wars and insurrections, do not be terrified; for such things must happen first, but it will not immediately be the end.' Then He said to them, 'nations will rise against nations, and kingdom against kingdom. There will be powerful earthquakes, famines, and plagues from place to place; and awesome sights and mighty signs will come from the sky. Before all this happens, however, they will seize and persecute you, they will hand you over to the synagogues and to prisons, and they will have you led before kings and governors because of My name. It will lead to your giving testimony. Remember, you are not to prepare your defense before-hand, for I myself shall give you a wisdom in speaking that all your adversaries will be powerless to resist or refute. You will be hated by all because of My name, but not a hair on your head will be destroyed. By your perseverance you will secure your lives."

In Hebrews 9:27 we read "Everyone must die once, and after that be judged by God." This is called Eschatology, or the four last things of our human life: Death, Judgment, Heaven or Hell. Jesus told us so often, "I am the way, the truth, and the life. Come follow Me!" So ends our International Year, but not our Revereies.

> "We strolled the lanes together,
> Laughed at the rains together,
> Your're gone from me
> But in my memory
> We always will be together."

"Since we are travelers and pilgrims in this world, let us ever ponder on the end of the road, that is of our life, for the end of our roadway is our home." (St. Columban)

GOD BLESS YOU ALL   **BERT HOFFMAN**

FINIS